UNDERSTANDING

Gabriele Ganz is Professor of L... Southampton.

J.A.G. Griffith is Emeritus Professor of Public Law in the University of London.

UNDERSTANDING LAW
Editor: J.A.G. Griffith

Understanding Contract Law
John Adams and Roger Brownsword

Understanding Criminal Law
C.M.V. Clarkson

Understanding Public Law
Gabriele Ganz

Understanding Equity and Trusts
Jeffrey Hackney

Understanding Tort Law
Carol Harlow

Understanding Property Law
W.T. Murphy and Simon Roberts

Gabriele Ganz

UNDERSTANDING
PUBLIC LAW

Second Edition

FontanaPress
An Imprint of HarperCollinsPublishers

Fontana Press
An Imprint of HarperCollins*Publishers*
77–85 Fulham Palace Road,
Hammersmith, London W6 8JB

Published by Fontana Press 1994
1 3 5 7 9 8 6 4 2

First Edition published in Great Britain by
Fontana Press 1987

Copyright © Gabriele Ganz 1987, 1994

Gabriele Ganz asserts the moral right to
be identified as the author of this work

ISBN 0 00 686296 9

Set in Times by Hewer Text Composition Services,
Edinburgh

Printed in Great Britain by
HarperCollinsManufacturing Glasgow

CONTENTS

EDITOR'S PREFACE

This series is directed primarily at two groups of readers: the general reader who wishes to understand what it is that lawyers are talking about and the law student who is told that he is about to study a subject called tort, or contract, or criminal law, or property, or trusts and equity, or public law. These titles convey little that is clear about the nature of their subjects and the extra-legal meanings that attach to some – such as contract or criminal law – may be misleading.

Each book in this series seeks to explain what the subject is about, what are the special kinds of problems it seeks to solve, and why it has developed as it has. The books are not at all meant to be summaries of their subjects, each of which covers a complicated area of human activity.

The law student will, in his or her course, be expected to read much longer and fuller texts on the subjects, to attend lectures and tutorials. The books in this series seek to provide introductions to be read early in the course or before it begins. It is hoped that these introductions will enable the student to grasp the essentials before coming to grips with the details. So also, the general reader who wishes to pursue the subject more fully will have to read the more detailed texts.

Although these books are intended to be introductions, they are not meant to be simplifications. These are not 'easy' books, however clearly they are written. Understanding law is not an easy matter. This is not, as is often said, primarily because lawyers use words with special meanings. It is because law has to deal with the complications, both personal and commercial, that people become involved in. We are all as busy as ants, more purposeful and sometimes less efficient. Law tries to regularize these complications and so cannot avoid being itself complicated.

The intention of the series will be achieved if the books give the reader a broad perspective and a general understanding of the legal principles on which these different subjects are based.

John Griffith

INTRODUCTION TO
THE FIRST EDITION

The British constitution used to be the envy of the world. The Westminster model was one of our main exports – now foreign institutions swell our growing range of imports. Great constitutional writers such as Bagehot (1867) and Dicey (1885) had no doubt that our constitution was superior to the American and French models. Today it is difficult to find any writer who is not critical of our institutions. There is hardly any element of the constitution which has not come under attack. Even the Queen or, more accurately, the functions she may still have to perform – i.e. choosing the Prime Minister and dissolving Parliament – have been subjected to much critical analysis in the light of the possibility of a hung Parliament. Lord Hailsham, when in opposition, condemned the system in its entirety as an 'Elective Dictatorship' and wanted to start afresh with a new constitution (Hailsham, 1976). Roy Jenkins in his Dimbleby lecture 'Home Thoughts from Abroad' laid all our ills at the feet of our electoral system and recommended proportional representation as a panacea (Jenkins, 1979). Richard Crossman (1975), Tony Benn (1980), John Mackintosh (1977) as well as others have pinpointed Prime Ministerial power as the root of all evil. Crossman and Benn have also been in the forefront of the attack on the Civil Service as usurpers of the power of elected governments. Since the Conservatives came to office, criticism has been augmented from the opposite end of the political spectrum which has been reinforced as a result of the leaks of information by Sarah Tisdall and Clive Ponting. The atrophy of the convention of ministerial responsibility to Parliament has been debated since the resignation of Sir Thomas Dugdale over the Crichel Down fiasco. The breakdown of collective responsibility of ministers was documented by the Franks review of the Falkland Islands (Cmnd 8787, 1983) and highlighted by the resignation of Michael Heseltine in the Westland Helicopters affair.

The functioning of Parliament has been under constant attack. Reform of the House of Lords has been on the political agenda all this century and abolition has been the official policy of the Labour Party. The working of the House of Commons, especially in the areas of legislation and control over finance, in spite of numerous reforms since the war is still regarded by its own members as in need of drastic change.

The secrecy of governments, and in particular the Official Secrets Act 1911, section 2 are almost universally execrated, and the call for a Freedom of Information Act becomes stronger every day. Similarly there has been much pressure for a Bill of Rights to safeguard the rights of the individual against encroachment by the government and Parliament. Carried to its logical conclusion this would challenge the sovereignty of Parliament, the cornerstone of the constitution. It would also involve the judiciary in political decision-making to a much greater degree than at present. The judiciary have not escaped attack for their more active role in controlling the power of public authorities.

The functioning of public authorities and in particular their relationship with each other − i.e. central–local relations and those between the government and nationalized industries − have ranged from a lack of harmony to complete breakdown in the case of some local authorities.

In the past decade or so referenda have been used twice to defuse constitutional issues and have been called for, unsuccessfully so far, to solve other constitutional problems.

The above is not a happy catalogue. Why is almost every aspect of our constitution under attack? Why is it no longer regarded as a model to be copied but as a disaster to be avoided? Is it the institutions which have changed or the people who work them or the people who are governed by them or the circumstances in which they operate? Has economic decline brought about political decline or vice versa? Has the very strength of our unwritten constitution become its weakness? Have the internal conventional safeguards broken down and should they be replaced by a written constitution containing legal safeguards? How could such a change be reconciled with representative democracy? Does such a system of government itself lead to elective dictatorship unless it is restrained by non-elected bodies? Or is our constitution not democratic enough? Should there be more participation by citizens in decision-making, e.g. by referenda, and more openness without which intelligent participation is impossible? Proportional representation would bring a closer correlation between votes and elected representatives. These approaches starting from opposite premises would each lead to a dilution of governmental power. The limits within which governmental power should be constrained is the ultimate question for any constitution. Whether these limits should be external or internal, legal or conventional is a question of means towards this end. Whether the constraints should be democratic or undemocratic is a question of ideology. Constitutional questions cannot be divorced from ideology. It is ideology that determines the content of the constitution. A constitution embodies an ideology, but in an unwritten constitution such as ours there is much flexibility. The same institutions, e.g. the Monarchy, can evolve to serve different ends, and those who work the institutions have much scope to mould them to their own ends, e.g. the Prime Minister.

A constitution cannot be divorced from the social and economic context in which it operates. Depending on these circumstances it may be subjected to strains and conflicts which test it to breaking point. A constitution cannot by itself solve social and economic problems though it may provide the mechanisms for their solution. No constitution can forestall an oil crisis but it can help to mitigate the problems arising therefrom. Economics and politics overlap but they are not coterminous.

All these issues underlie a discussion of the constitution as it exists today. Such a discussion is as difficult as taking a snapshot of a changing panorama or trying to hit a moving target because the subject matter is constantly evolving, sometimes imperceptibly. All constitutions must be able to change if they are not to break and written constitutions usually provide special procedures for this purpose. Our constitution, which is not embodied in one or more documents, is more flexible than almost any other for two reasons. First, so far as it is embodied in legal rules, these can be changed by an Act of Parliament in the same way that any other law can be changed. Secondly, the essence of the British constitution lies not in its laws but in its conventions, i.e. in rules which do not have the force of law but which have evolved gradually and continue to do so and have transformed the constitution behind the legal facade. These two hallmarks of the constitution, the sovereignty of Parliament and the conventions of the constitution, have not escaped the wave of criticism but have been central targets for the attackers. Lord Hailsham put sovereignty of Parliament in the forefront of his indictment because Parliament is 'absolute and unlimited'. This led him to call for legal limits in a written constitution. Similarly the breakdown of conventions relating to the conduct of the Prime Minister, other ministers, the Civil Service and the relationship between central and local government has led to calls by Lord Scarman (1985) for a written constitution as a remedy. These attacks are aimed at the twin pillars of the constitution which must now be evaluated.

INTRODUCTION TO
THE SECOND EDITION

Much water has flowed under bridges since the first edition of this book. Then the constitution was under discussion, now the reform of the constitution has become a growth industry. Blueprints for constitutional reform have become a flood. The Institute for Public Policy Research has drawn up a full-blown written Constitution of the United Kingdom (1991), the Liberal Democrats have drafted a similar document (1990), whilst the Labour party has wide-ranging plans for reform as well as setting up the Plant Committee on Electoral Reform which has issued its final report (1993). Charter 88, a pressure group for constitutional reform, has around 50,000 supporters for its programme and Tony Benn presented his radical Commonwealth of Britain Bill to the House of Commons in May 1991 (HC Deb., vol. 191, col. 666, 20 May 1991). Books on constitutional reform proliferate, ranging from academic lawyers such as Brazier's *Constitutional Reform* (1991) and Oliver's *Government in the United Kingdom* (1991), to a former head of Mrs Thatcher's policy unit, Ferdinand Mount's *The British Constitution Now* (1992). Only the Conservative government has no proposals for change, which is not surprising after its fourth election victory in 1992.

This fourth victory, unprecedented since 1826, is perhaps the most potent reason for constitutional reform. A democracy where a party with a majority in the House of Commons can pass its policies into law with very few obstructions is in Lord Hailsham's felicitous phrase an 'elective dictatorship' (Hailsham, 1976). If elections can no longer produce an alternative government, as seems possible, especially after a further Parliamentary Boundary

Review which is being brought forward to 1994 (Boundary Commissions Act 1992), it is in danger of becoming a dictatorship pure and simple. A *coup d'état* within the governing party then becomes the only mechanism for change, which is what happened when Mrs Thatcher was toppled as Prime Minister in November 1990 in a Conservative leadership election, when the unpopularity of the poll tax was at its height.

The danger to British parliamentary democracy of one-party government for the foreseeable future is all the greater because it has traditionally been held in check by conventional rather than legal rules. Individual ministerial responsibility has atrophied further since the first edition, though collective decision-making has probably been strengthened since the advent of Mr Major as Prime Minister.

The same cannot be said of the civil service whose political neutrality and independence are increasingly being replaced by contracting out to the private sector and by the creation of executive agencies whose accountability to Parliament is still in its infancy.

The House of Commons has been emasculated even further. The guillotining of legislation has reached an all-time high and threatens to become automatic. The setting up of Select Committees after the 1992 General Election saw the ousting of the rebellious Conservative MP Nicholas Winterton, to the dismay of MPs on both sides of the House but without the government being defeated over the issue (HC Deb., vol. 211, col. 913, 13 July 1992). In contrast they did suffer a rare defeat over the size of the increase in MPs' office cost allowances (HC Deb., vol. 211, col. 1081, 14 July 1992).

The House of Lords continued to be a thorn in the flesh of the government but did not cover themselves in glory by rejecting the War Crimes Bill 1991 which became the first Act to be passed under the Parliament Act 1949. Increasingly Acts are becoming skeleton legislation giving blanket powers to ministers to lay down not the details but the policy itself, which has given rise to severe but helpless criticism from the courts who cannot override the will of Parliament.

Throughout administrative decision-making there has been a streamlining in the interests of economy and efficiency at the expense of fairness and impartiality. This has to be seen in the context of the Citizen's Charter, 1991 (Cm 1599) which views the citizen as a consumer of public services who is entitled to efficiency in their delivery and compensation for their failure. The Charter also applies to the privatized public utilities within which it is intended to include the remaining state-owned industries. The government's announcement of British Coal's proposal to close over thirty pits led to an outcry which forced a review and some modification of the policy but 18 months later, more than this number had been closed prior to privatization.

The other public sector bodies under threat are local authorities which are now seen by the government not as providing public services themselves but as enabling others, in particular the private sector, to deliver them. This is the philosophy underpinning yet another reorganization which local government is undergoing.

The status of civil liberties has not been enhanced since the first edition. The Official Secrets Act 1989 narrows the scope of the 1911 Act but is even more draconian, particularly as regards disclosures by members of the security services. Though MI5 and MI6 have been put on a statutory basis by the Security Service Act 1989 and the Intelligence Services Act 1994 and the heads of both services have been named, their accountability still leaves much to be desired.

Mr Major has made some concessions to open government such as the publication of the standing Cabinet Committees (HC Deb., vol. 208, col. 110, Written Answers, 19 May 1992) and a Code of Practice on Open Government (1994) but this still falls a long way short of a Freedom of Information Act giving a statutory right of access to official papers.

A Royal Commission on Criminal Justice set up in 1991, the first Royal Commission since 1979, reported in 1993 (Cm 2263). This followed the overturning of the convictions of the Guildford 4 and the Birmingham 6 as well as many other miscarriages of justice, some of which occurred after safeguards for suspects in police custody were introduced by the Police and

Criminal Evidence Act 1984. The Criminal Justice and Public Order Bill 1994 rejected one of its key recommendations by amending the right of silence. This Bill has also added a host of offences relating to collective trespass and nuisance on land to those contained in the earlier Public Order Act 1986 which has not prevented further outbreaks of violence in the inner cities but has been used to clear away would-be worshippers from Stonehenge and 'New Age' travellers who trespass on private land.

Even the Queen, who celebrated the 40th anniversary of her accession in 1992, was under attack for her immunity from taxation and for the inflation-proofed Civil List payments granted to her in 1990 for the next ten years (HC Deb., vol. 177, col. 299, 24 July 1990). She has now agreed to pay income tax on her personal income and to refund the cost of all the annuities paid to members of the royal family except that of the Queen Mother and the Duke of Edinburgh (HC Deb., vol. 218, col. 1111, 11 February 1993). The separation of the Prince and Princess of Wales was said by the Prime Minister to have no constitutional implications (HC Deb., vol. 215, col. 845, 9 December 1992) but this remains to be seen. Certainly the 'annus horribilis' of 1992 has rocked the monarchy to its foundations.

Perhaps most importantly from a strictly constitutional perspective is the open recognition by the House of Lords in the *Factortame* Case (1990) of the demise of the sovereignty of Parliament, the fundamental principle of the constitution, as a result of the United Kingdom's accession to the European Community by the European Communities Act 1972. The Act enacting the Maastricht Treaty signed in February 1992 took the whole first session of the new Parliament and was only finally disposed of by a vote of confidence to quell the rebellion of Conservative Euro-sceptics. Not even Baroness Thatcher could rally sufficient support for a clause requiring a referendum to be held on the Treaty.

Devolution of powers to Scotland and Wales, on which referenda were held in 1979, has been rejected by Mr Major as have other proposals for constitutional reforms such as a Bill of

Rights, reform of the House of Lords, electoral reform and above all a written constitution.

The future, therefore, looks bleak for constitutional reform. Not only will a government who benefits from the absence of checks and balances refuse to change the system but the prospect of changing the government is problematic. The only possibilities for change in the near future come from the European Union which is becoming ever more important in our domestic affairs or from inside the Conservative party. If opposition from Conservative MPs is combined with the opposition, defeat of the government is possible. The danger arises when a government exercising unrestrained power can no longer be removed by constitutional means.

ELECTIVE DICTATORSHIP

The extent to which the perception of the British constitution has changed over the last hundred years is well illustrated by quotations from Dicey's *Law of the Constitution* (1885) and Lord Hailsham's lecture 'Elective Dictatorship' (1976). First, Dicey on sovereignty: 'The essential property of representative government is to produce coincidence between the wishes of the sovereign and the wishes of the subjects . . . This, which is true in its nature of all real representative government, applies with special truth to the English House of Commons' (p. 84). On conventions, Dicey said: 'The conventions of the constitution now consist of customs which (whatever their historical origin) are at the present day maintained for the sake of ensuring the supremacy of the House of Commons and, ultimately, through the elective House of Commons, of the nation' (pp. 430–1). Contrast these quotations with Lord Hailsham: 'So the sovereignty of Parliament has increasingly become, in practice, the sovereignty of the Commons, and the sovereignty of the Commons has increasingly become the sovereignty of the government, which in addition to its influence in Parliament, controls the party whips, the party machine and the civil service. This means that what has always been an elective dictatorship in theory, but one in which the component parts operated, in practice, to control one another, has become a machine in which one of those parts has come to exercise a predominant influence over the rest' (p. 497). And more succinctly: 'The government controls Parliament and not Parliament the government' (p. 496). So the nub of the indictment is that the elected part of Parliament, namely the

House of Commons, having achieved supremacy over the un-elected parts, namely the Queen and the House of Lords, has surrendered its sovereignty to the government which controls it through the party machine.

Which of these snapshots represents a more accurate picture of the constitution as it exists today? If the aim of representative government is 'to produce coincidence between the wishes of the sovereign and the wishes of the subjects' the representative body must reflect the wishes of the electorate and exercise control over the government. The crucial issues, therefore, are the electoral system and the relationship between the government and Parliament.

ELECTORAL SYSTEM

Historically the electoral system is based on the representation of communities. This is still reflected in the qualification for voting and the method of voting. Everyone who is 18, a Commonwealth citizen or a citizen of Eire (and soon a citizen of the European Union), not a peer and not serving a sentence of imprisonment is entitled to be placed on the electoral register in a constituency where he is resident on October 10 (Representation of the People Act 1983). Though residence does not now involve a qualifying period it does require a considerable degree of permanence (*Hipperson v. Newbury Electoral Registration Officer*, 1985) which even today can disenfranchise the homeless and 'New Age' travellers. Also some places, e.g. mental institutions and prisons, may not be treated as residences. Those who cannot satisfy the residence qualification may be entitled to be registered in a constituency where they were resident, e.g. if they are absent because they are members of the armed forces or British citizens living abroad who have been registered there within the preceding 20 years (Representation of the People Act 1989). In such cases entitlement to vote is based on citizenship rather than residence to which lip-service is paid through registration in the constituency where the citizen was previously resident. Such a notional residence is essential as all voters must be on an electoral roll in a constituency.

The constituency is the linchpin of our electoral system. Its origin lies in the representation of communities which is still an important part of an MP's work. There is, however, a constant tension between this concept of representation and the modern party system which affects so many facets of our representative democracy. It manifests itself at the outset when the constituency boundaries are drawn. These are now reviewed every eight to twelve years (Boundary Commissions Act 1992) by four politically impartial Boundary Commissions, one for each part of the United Kingdom (Parliamentary Constituencies Act 1986). Their terms of reference enjoin them to create constituencies as near as possible to the electoral quota which is obtained by dividing the electorate of that part of the United Kingdom by the number of constituencies in it without crossing county or London borough boundaries (unless these are exceptional circumstances) and taking into account local ties. The number of seats has increased with each review and is now 651 but the changes in population are not evenly spread throughout the country. This has profound implications for the political parties but political considerations cannot be taken into account by the Commissions and, therefore, political arguments are put to them cloaked in arguments about local ties (Home Affairs Committee Report, HC 97 (1986–7), p. 80). Not surprisingly each review since 1945 has given rise to political controversy. In 1969 the Labour government refused to implement the Boundary Commissions' recommendations and in 1983 unsuccessfully challenged them in Court (*R. v. Boundary Commission for England ex parte Foot*, 1983).

The crucial importance of constituency boundaries to the outcome of elections is the result of our electoral system, called first past the post, under which an MP is elected for a constituency if he receives one vote more than his nearest rival however small his percentage of the total vote. This not only enables MPs to be elected on a minority vote (over 250 MPs in 1992) but on two occasions since the war (1951 and February 1974) the party gaining most seats polled fewer votes than the main opposition party. Most disadvantaged by our electoral system are the Liberal Democrats, whose support is fairly evenly spread throughout the country and who come second in a large number of seats (154 seats in 1992) but only win a handful of seats where their support is concentrated. In 1992 they gained twenty seats for 18% of the vote, whilst Labour gained 271 seats for 34% and the Conservatives 336 seats with 42% of the vote. It is this glaring discrepancy between seats and votes since the revival of the Liberal party in 1974 which has fuelled the pressure for electoral reform.

Britain is the only country in the European Union which uses the first past the post system. There are a number of alternative systems. The Alternative Vote retains single member constituencies but voters list candidates in order of preference and it ensures that an MP is elected by more than 50% of the voters including second-preference votes. The most proportional system, i.e. the one which matches seats to votes cast most accurately, is the list system where the vote is cast for a party which is allocated seats in proportion to the votes cast with the possibility of requiring a party to obtain a minimum percentage of votes. The seats are then filled from candidates on the party list. The Single Transferable Vote where voting is for candidates in order of preference in multi-member constituencies is less proportional than the list system but more proportional than the Alternative Vote. To choose between these systems and the existing one or to decide which system to adopt involves complex questions (The Plant Report 1991). The most fundamental issue is the purpose of elections. Are they intended to represent the party preferences of voters as accurately as possible, in which case the list system is the best buy, or are they intended to choose a stable government? In the latter case under the present party system in Britain the first past the post system is most likely to produce a government with a majority of seats in the House of Commons. Any other system would be more likely to lead to a hung Parliament where no party has a majority and where the third party holds the balance of power.

The choice between the existing electoral system and more proportional systems is now not only a matter of balancing the merits of majority governments against the alternative. The

4

alternation between majority governments which has been an implicit assumption of our system of government is now being called into question. The fourth successive victory of the Conservatives in 1992 raises the spectre of the one-party state where one party is permanently in government and the others are permanently in opposition. This scenario is under-pinned by social change and demographic distribution of the votes of the two main parties with Labour's support concentrated in Scotland, Wales and the North of England and in the inner cities whilst Conservative support lies in the South. In the 1992 election Labour won only 10 seats out of 177 outside London and south of a line from the Wash to the Bristol Channel. As the population movement is from the North to the South and out of the cities into the countryside, it is inevitable that Labour loses seats at every redrawing of constituency boundaries however impartially carried out, though this is not expected to be as significant in the current review. Where one-party dominance is inevitable under a first past the post system as in Northern Ireland or in Scotland, if either were again to be given their own legislative assemblies, it has been accepted that proportional representation must be used to avoid a permanent majority of one party (Northern Ireland Constitution Act 1973, section 29) and similarly, proposals for a Scottish Assembly now accept that it must be elected by a system of proportional representation. The time may have come when similar facts dictate the same choice in the United Kingdom as a whole. There is only one proportional system of voting, i.e. where seats are allocated in proportion to votes, which retains the link between an MP and his constituents in single-member constituencies. This is the Additional Member System used in Germany where half the members of the Bundestag are elected on the first past the post system and the other half of the seats are distributed in accordance with the votes cast for the party so as to achieve proportionality – each voter having two votes, one for a constituency MP and one for the party. Such a system or a variant upon it has been suggested for the United Kingdom by some constitutional reformers including the Hansard Society Commission on Electoral Reform (1976) but not by the final Plant Report (1993).

5

It would safeguard an important function of MPs to redress the grievances of their constituents but like other proportional electoral systems it would most probably prevent a party obtaining an overall majority of seats.

CHOICE OF PRIME MINISTER

This brings us to the choice of Prime Minister who heads the government. In law it is the Queen who appoints the Prime Minister; in practice she must appoint the leader of the party which has won the majority of seats in the House of Commons. This forms the crucial link between the government and Parliament. If a party wins an overall majority of seats the choice of Prime Minister is clear but even under the present electoral system this did not happen in February 1974, and if proportional representation were to be adopted it would become the exception rather than the norm. Where no party obtains a clear majority there are no legal rules, only conventional rules based on past precedents, which may not give a definitive answer because the situation is not identical and the rules are flexible. This flexibility would be lost if the rules were embodied in a written constitution. Ultimately the decision lies with the Queen and her advisers, though politicians will, if at all possible, settle the problem among themselves. What is the problem?

If the Prime Minister, who remains in office during the General Election, loses his overall majority he may try, as Mr Heath did in 1974, to form a coalition with another party in order to obtain such a majority. If he fails he should resign, as Mr Heath did, whether or not his party has won more seats than any other party (as Mr Heath's did not in 1974). For the only alternative to resignation would be to ask the Queen to dissolve Parliament again and hold another election; and for this there is no precedent. The leader of the party with the next highest number of seats should, therefore, be asked to form a government. Unless he forms a coalition and obtains an overall majority he will be in a minority and risk defeat in the House of Commons. If this happens very soon, at the end of the debate on the Queen's speech, the problem arises whether he is entitled to ask the Queen to dissolve Parliament or whether she could refuse his request and ask the leader of the third party to try to form a government. In 1974 the minority Labour government was not defeated in this way and the Prime Minister did not ask for a dissolution until eight months had elapsed after the previous General Election. Whichever action the Queen took would involve her in controversy. To refuse the Prime Minister a dissolution would be unprecedented in modern times. To grant one so soon after the previous election would not only be undesirable but might lay her open to charges of partiality if she had already refused one to the outgoing Prime Minister. The only way out of this dilemma is for the parties to reach agreement among themselves either by forming a coalition or, if this is not possible, to allow a minority government a breathing space in which to govern, as happened in 1974.

A similar problem would arise if a coalition government had been formed and one of the partners left the government so that it no longer had a majority in the House of Commons. If the Prime Minister of the minority government were to ask the Queen for a dissolution of Parliament could she refuse if the party who left the government now supported the opposition who thus had a majority in the House of Commons? This happened in Germany in 1982 but, unlike Germany, we have no constitution which regulates such a situation. The convention that the Queen must act on the advice of the Prime Minister conflicts with that which obliges her to appoint as Prime Minister the person who commands a majority in the Commons. Once again, to refuse a dissolution would involve the Queen in controversy whereas to grant one would only do so if it was very soon after a General Election or it was in war-time or at a time of national emergency.

The appointment of a Prime Minister may also arise when the existing one dies or resigns from office. The Conservatives did not elect their leader until 1965, so that when Harold Macmillan resigned as Prime Minister in 1963, the Queen was at least formally involved in the controversy surrounding the choice of a successor. The three main parties have very different rules for the election of a leader. The Liberal Democrat leader is elected by all the members of the party. Since 1981 the Labour leader is elected by an electoral college consisting of Labour MPs (one-third), the constituency Labour parties (one-third) and the trade unions (one-third) with voting taking place on the basis of one member-one vote.. This could at some future time cause constitutional problems if the leader so chosen was not acceptable to Labour MPs on whose loyalty a Labour Prime Minister would depend. The electorate for the Conservative leader consists effectively of Conservative MPs but the procedure is a complex one and made constitutional history when it was used in November 1990 to oust Mrs Thatcher as Prime Minister.

The uniqueness of what happened in 1990 lies in the fact that the Prime Minister lost office not as a result of an election defeat or the break up of a coalition government or being forced to resign due to ill-health or a vote in the House of Commons, nor was it a voluntary retirement. Mrs Thatcher was the first Prime Minister to be voted out of office by MPs of her own party. This could only happen because there is provision in the rules of the Conservative party since 1975 for an annual election whether the party is in office or not. A Labour Prime Minister can only be challenged at the Party conference if a majority on a card vote calls for an election. In 1990 it only needed a proposer and seconder whose names were not published to nominate a rival candidate. Since then the rules have been changed to require an election to be requested by 10% of Conservative MPs before nominations can be made and the names of the proposer and seconder now have to be published. Mrs Thatcher received an overall majority but fell short by 4 votes of the 15% of those entitled to vote by which she had to exceed her nearest rival. At the last minute she withdrew from the second ballot for which only an absolute majority of those entitled to vote is needed. Mr Major fell 2 votes short of an absolute majority but his nearest rival, Mr Heseltine, conceded defeat. If neither happens a third ballot will have to be held.

The constitutional significance of these events is that they illustrate very graphically that a Prime Minister can be dismissed without a General Election as has happened on previous occasions through resignations forced or otherwise. More importantly, in the context of whether Britain is an elective dictatorship, it shows that there are constitutional mechanisms other than a General Election for removing the alleged dictator. This is very relevant to the debate about whether we have Prime Ministerial or Cabinet government which will now be examined.

PRIME MINISTER'S POWERS

Appointment and dismissal of ministers

The first and perhaps foremost power of the Prime Minister is that of appointing and dismissing ministers. In law, appointments are made by the Queen; by convention the power is exercised on the advice of the Prime Minister. The most important constitutional constraint, which again has grown up through convention, is that ministers must be or become members of either the House of Commons or the House of Lords. The holders of the most important offices (including the Prime Ministership itself) normally sit in the Commons, though there have been some notable recent exceptions such as Lord Carrington (Minister of Defence and Foreign Secretary) and Lord Young (Employment Secretary). The most important officeholders and other ministers of the Prime Minister's choosing are appointed members of the Cabinet which normally has between twenty and twenty-five members. This is the body which Bagehot (1867, p.68) called 'a *hyphen* which joins, a *buckle* which fastens, the legislative part of the State to the executive part of the State'.

There are, of course, political constraints on the Prime Minister in appointing ministers. Senior members of the governing party, e.g. those who sat on the opposition front bench, will have a prior claim to be considered. But the situation would be transformed if, as Mr Benn (1980) has suggested, the Cabinet were elected by the MPs of the party in power in the same way as Labour MPs elect their Shadow Cabinet which, in accordance with Standing Orders of the Labour Party, has to become the Cabinet when Labour wins the election. The power of the Prime Minister would be curtailed even more drastically by his suggestion for annual elections, for this would take away the power of dismissal, which is the most potent instrument for moulding the Cabinet to the Prime Minister's will. The limits on this power are personal and political. Some Prime Ministers are more ruthless than others. The political constraints involve balancing the risks of opposition from the ex-minister on the back benches with those from keeping him within the Cabinet. Mr Benn was never dismissed from the Labour Cabinet, while Mrs Thatcher steadily eliminated her opponents from her government. Mr Macmillan dismissed seven Cabinet ministers at one time in 1962. The political repercussions of such actions may not be immediately apparent. The penalty may not be paid until the next election in lost popularity. Before then it may lead to more opposition from the government back benches. In the case of Mrs Thatcher former Cabinet ministers played a leading part in her downfall.

Relationship between Prime Minister and Cabinet

The relationship between the Prime Minister and his Cabinet is also very much a matter of personalities, both his and theirs. The proponents of Prime Ministerial power point to the power to control the agenda of Cabinet meetings, the use of Cabinet committees appointed by the Prime Minister or informal groups of ministers instead of the full Cabinet for decision-making, the power derived from presiding over the Cabinet and summing up its discussions, and the close relationship with the Secretary to the Cabinet who is also the Head of the Civil Service. Each Prime Minister uses these powers differently and since Cabinet proceedings are held in secret we have to rely on the conflicting accounts of the participants after the event and unattributable leaks at the time. After thirty years Cabinet documents are made public (Public Records Acts 1958 and 1967). Exceptionally Cabinet documents may be made available to a committee of inquiry as happened in the case of the Franks review of the Falkland Islands (Cmnd 8787, 1983). Even more exceptionally, Cabinet secrets may be openly bandied about in the press and the House of

Commons as happened in the controversy over the rescue of the Westland Helicopter Company. From these sources it is becoming increasingly clear that the Cabinet is no longer the strategic decision-making body which is implied in the phrase 'Cabinet government'. Not only is the agenda pre-empted by routine business and one-off cases which could not be resolved elsewhere but some very important issues have not been discussed there. These include Britain's atom bomb under Attlee, the Suez intervention by Eden, devaluation of the pound by Wilson, and, under Mrs Thatcher, the Falklands issue prior to the Argentine invasion, the banning of trade unions at GCHQ, the granting of consent to the USA to use its British bases for the bombing of Libya, and the rescue of the Westland Helicopter Company. It was Mrs Thatcher's refusal to allow this last issue to be discussed in Cabinet that led Mr Heseltine, the Defence Secretary, to charge Mrs Thatcher with responsibility for 'the breakdown of constitutional government' (*Observer*, 12 January 1986). The former Prime Minister, Mr Callaghan, thought this was overegging the pudding and put the blame squarely on the Cabinet. It was up to them to decide what they would put up with. 'If they behave like mice they must expect to be chased' (HC Deb., vol. 89, col. 1115, 15 January 1986). The ultimate weapon that a member of the Cabinet can use if he does not approve of what is being done in or outside the Cabinet is to resign, as Mr Heseltine did, but the weapon may turn out to be a boomerang.

COLLECTIVE RESPONSIBILITY

When a minister resigns because of disagreement with the Prime Minister and his colleagues he is observing the convention of collective responsibility. According to this rule of the constitution, each member of the government must support the government's decisions inside Parliament and outside. The corollary of this rule is Cabinet secrecy. The public unanimity would be exposed as a sham if the private disagreements were immediately revealed, or they would not be expressed if the participants knew in advance that they would be revealed publicly later. These considerations become weaker with the lapse of time. Though the thirty-year rule marks the legal termination of secrecy, fifteen years has been accepted as a conventional guideline for disclosure by ministers of confidential Cabinet discussions (Cmnd 6386, 1976). This followed the unsuccessful attempt to stop the publication of the sensational Crossman *Diaries* which revealed the inner workings of Mr Wilson's first government ten years later when Labour was again in power (*AG v. Jonathan Cape Ltd*, 1976). Both the unanimity rule and the secrecy rule have been more honoured in the breach than the observance. The rationale of the convention is to strengthen the government in whom public confidence is undermined by the exposure of open disagreements. But there have been occasions when open disagreement has been the only mechanism to prevent the government splitting apart and the convention has been deliberately set aside by an agreement to differ. This happened for the first time in 1932 in the case of a coalition government but it did not prevent the dissenting ministers resigning shortly afterwards. Mr Wilson followed this precedent in 1975, allowing open disagreement between members of the government over the government's recommendation to remain in the EEC, during the referendum campaign (HC Deb., vol. 889, col. 351, Written Answers, 7 April 1975). He did not extend this freedom to parliamentary proceedings and dismissed Mr Heffer for breaking this rule. Mr Callaghan set aside the convention in 1977 when allowing a free vote on a government Bill providing for direct elections to the European Assembly but did not extend this freedom to speaking against the Bill. When asked about this decision he made the revealing remark, 'I certainly think that the doctrine should apply, except in cases where I announce that it does not' (HC Deb., vol. 933, col. 552, 16 June 1977). Is the unanimity and secrecy convention a rule the Prime Minister can use or not to strengthen his position? The waiver of the rule can be seen in this light but it can also be regarded as a desperate remedy to prevent the government from disintegrating.

Unattributable leaks relating to Cabinet discussions are another safety-valve to preserve the façade of unanimity while at the same time allowing the hidden disagreements to surface without the source being revealed. These leaks may come from the Prime Minister as well as from dissenting ministers. Again Mr Callaghan spoke memorably: 'You know the difference between leaking and briefing. Briefing is what I do and leaking is what you do' (Cmnd 5104, vol. 4, p. 187, 1972).

Leaking still pays lip service to the rule, open disagreement between ministers breaks it. No Prime Minister can welcome this; it is a sign of weakness, not strength. To assert his authority, the Prime Minister must try to silence the minister or dismiss him. It was Mrs Thatcher's ultimatum to Mr Heseltine to observe collective responsibility in the Westland Helicopters affair that precipitated his walk-out from the Cabinet after retorting that he would accept collective responsibility where there had been collective decision-making. This correlation has not existed since the classic days of Cabinet government described by Bagehot. The unanimity rule has long been extended beyond members of the Cabinet and, as we have seen, the Cabinet is no longer the sole decision-making body. The acceleration of this trend under Mrs Thatcher was the basic constitutional issue raised by Mr Heseltine. There seems to have been a return to more collective decision-making under John Major but the decision to close down over 30 pits with the loss of 30,000 mining jobs was taken by key ministers in economic departments but without the approval of the Cabinet (*The Times*, 16 October 1992).

The other aspect of collective responsibility, namely responsibility to the House of Commons, is the fulcrum on which our parliamentary democracy turns. The House of Commons holds the power of life and death over the government but equally the Prime Minister can destroy Parliament by asking for a dissolution. The government can govern only so long as it does not lose the support of the House of Commons. If it does, today, in contrast to the earlier part of the nineteenth century, this would inevitably lead to a General Election. Again, in contrast to the earlier part of the nineteenth century, we have a rigid party system with strict discipline and loyalty. A government which holds a majority in the House of Commons can only be defeated as a result of a revolt by its own backbenchers, who know that a successful revolt will place their own seats in jeopardy at the ensuing General Election. It is not, therefore, surprising that the only two governments to be defeated on a vote of confidence this century have been minority governments, both Labour governments in 1924 and 1979. If the Leader of the Opposition puts down a motion of no confidence the government must by convention provide time for its early debate. The government may also itself seek a vote of confidence or deliberately make an issue one of confidence in order to put the maximum pressure on its supporters, though it is at the same time putting its life in their hands. It can also use a vote of confidence on an issue to reverse a previous defeat on the issue or alternatively it can accept the defeat. In the past a defeat on a major issue was regarded as a matter of confidence but governments no longer treat them as such. This development has enabled governments, in particular minority governments, to survive longer but it has also enabled backbenchers, especially rebel government backbenchers, to score victories against the government.

It is also possible to have a hidden vote of confidence. This happened on 4 November, 1992 (HC Deb., vol. 213, col. 283) on the European Communities (Amendment) Bill which enacts the Maastricht Treaty into UK law. The Bill had been halted by the 'No' vote in the Danish referendum and the government had promised a further debate before continuing with the Bill. In order to rally the maximum support from the Euro-sceptic MPs in the Conservative party the government privately signalled the vote as one of confidence but publicly put down an anodyne motion to proceed with the Bill. The Labour opposition treated the vote as one of confidence in the government and voted against the motion whilst the Liberal Democrats supported the motion. The government scraped home by 3 votes after much arm-twisting and last minute concessions to its rebel MPs (Baker, Gamble and Ludlam 1993, p. 151). In the end the government was forced to bring its rebels into line on the Maastricht Treaty by an explicit vote of confidence (see below p. 49).

The convention of collective responsibility, the linchpin of our democracy, has thus contracted considerably in scope. It is now analogous to the ultimate deterrent whose fall-out is as lethal to those who use it as to those against whom it is used. The parallel convention of the individual responsibility of ministers has also undergone fundamental change.

INDIVIDUAL RESPONSIBILITY

The responsibility of individual ministers to the House of Commons can ultimately be enforced by the same mechanism as the collective responsibility of the government, namely by a vote of no confidence or censure. Though such a vote is not strictly one of confidence in the government, such a motion put down by the opposition will make the government side close ranks, and party discipline and loyalty will make the result a foregone conclusion. Individual responsibility is, therefore, brought about by other means. One must distinguish the responsibility of a minister for a matter of policy, for his personal behaviour and for the mistakes of his Department, though these do not form watertight categories.

Individual responsibility of ministers for policy matters merges into collective responsibility, for if the government disassociates itself from the policy of one of its members it is asserting collective responsibility in the same way as when a minister resigns because of policy disagreements with his colleagues. The resignation of Sir Samuel Hoare as Foreign Secretary in 1935, when the government repudiated the Hoare–Laval pact ceding Abyssinia to Italy because of the public outcry, can be seen as an example of such a resignation. However, the government had to admit to an error of judgement in first accepting the proposals, an error for which they did not offer to resign. Hoare was thus made a scapegoat for what was in effect a collective decision. Lord Carrington's resignation after the Argentine invasion of the Falkland Islands can be characterized in a similar way, for the policy prior to that invasion was that of the government and the resignation was made deliberately to conduct the lightning away from the government. Mr Lamont's resignation as Chancellor of the Exchequer can only be explained on the same lines. The Prime Minister congratulated him on his performance and said there would be no change in policy. But unlike Lord Carrington, Mr Lamont did not resign as a matter of honour, accepting responsibility for the government as a whole. He was removed in response to pressure from inside and outside the Conservative party to expiate the policy failure of the government (HC Deb., vol. 226, col. 279, 9 June 1993). Individual responsibility is here acting as a substitute for collective responsibility.

There is a similar blurring between individual and collective responsibility where the personal behaviour of a minister is under attack. The resignation of such a minister depends very much on the attitude of his colleagues and particularly that of the Prime Minister, though they are of course subject to outside pressures. Where the misconduct of the minister is not very serious, the Prime Minister can refuse to accept his resignation and thus condone his conduct, as happened in the case of Mr Robert Dunn, a junior Education Minister whose entry in *Who's Who* was misleading about his academic qualifications (*Guardian*, 9 May 1986). In effect he was protected with the shield of collective responsibility. If the public is sufficiently outraged this may not be politically possible. This happened in the case of Mr Cecil Parkinson. Mrs Thatcher stood by him at first when the affair with his secretary became public after the General Election of 1983. But after her revelations to *The Times* the public outcry and pressure within the party forced Mrs Thatcher to accept his resignation. Embarrassment to the government and the party also finally led to the resignation of Mr David Mellor over his affair with an actress and accepting free holidays, after an initial stand supported by the Prime Minister against being hounded from office by newspapers using unethical methods of investigation (Doig, 1993). Mr Mates' resignation over his involvement with Mr Nadir must now be added to this list (HC Deb., vol. 227 col. 823, 29 June 1993). Similarly Mr Macmillan could not have shielded Mr Profumo, who lied to the House over his affair with Christine Keeler. That a Prime Minister cannot always save a minister whose personal conduct is under attack is well illustrated by Mr Brittan's resignation over his leaking of a confidential letter from the Solicitor-General to Mr Heseltine during the Westland Helicopters affair. As Mr Brittan wrote in his resignation letter, he could no longer command the full confidence of his colleagues once he had been identified as the leaker, even though, as Mrs Thatcher wrote in her reply (in words similar to those in her reply to Lord Carrington's resignation), she had tried her utmost to dissuade him from resigning (*Guardian*, 25 January 1986). These cases demonstrate the limits on Prime Ministerial power to save a minister, limits imposed by public opinion, by colleagues collectively and by the sense of honour of individual ministers.

It has been argued that similar considerations apply to the responsibility of a minister for mistakes made by his Department (Finer, 1956, p. 394). The resignation of Sir Thomas Dugdale in 1954 over mismanagement in his Department of the sale of a piece of land called Crichel Down is the classic and arguably the last illustration of a minister resigning for the faults of his civil servants of which he neither knew nor could have known. A former colleague, Lord Boyle (1980, p.10), has claimed that Dugdale resigned because he stood by his decision rather than for the misconduct of his officials. His resignation was certainly not required according to the rules laid down by the Home Secretary in the debate on the matter (HC Deb., vol. 530, col. 1285, 20 July 1954). The civil servants were not carrying out his orders or acting in accordance with his policy. He did not have to defend the misconduct of his officials but he had to render an account to Parliament of his stewardship. Mr Prior rejected the Crichel Down case as a precedent when he was under pressure to resign after the mass break-out from the Maze Prison in Northern Ireland. He argued that it was not his policy that was to blame but failures in carrying out security procedures at the prison (HC Deb., vol. 53, col. 1041, 9 February 1984). This distinction between policy and administration was strongly criticized by MPs but it is difficult not to agree with the verdict of his junior minister that the constitutional convention requiring ministerial resignation in such a case 'had not existed in politics in this country for many years' (ibid., col. 1108). Mr Baker took a similar line over the escape of IRA suspects from Brixton prison and refused to resign (HC Deb., vol. 194, col. 649, 8 July 1991).

CIVIL SERVICE

The convention of ministerial responsibility regulates not only the relationship between ministers and the House of Commons but conversely that between ministers and civil servants. Civil servants are not elected but appointed officials who are responsible to their ministers. They advise ministers on the formulation of policy and carry it out. As a corollary they are normally protected by anonymity and are politically neutral, serving each government in turn. This relationship has been subjected to great strains recently and its hallmarks are being challenged and eroded by both ministers and civil servants.

The bedrock of political neutrality on which our permanent civil service is anchored has been threatened from several directions. Civil servants are recruited through open competition by, or under the supervision of, independent Civil Service Commissioners. However, in recent years ministers and particularly the Prime Minister have been more involved in promotion to senior posts and there have been appointments of outsiders to such posts. Mrs Thatcher was widely credited with asking whether the appointee was 'one of us'. This did not mean someone who was a Conservative but a person in tune with the style and ethos of the government. Since most Permanent Secretaries, who are the civil servants heading government departments, have been appointed since 1979, when the Conservatives came to power, this has profound significance for a subsequent government of a different party political complexion. More worrying is the recent removal of a Permanent Secretary, Sir Peter Kemp, because his face no longer fitted and he was not acceptable to his political master (HC 390-I, 1992–3, para. 36).

This problem is not limited to the top echelons of the civil service but permeates down the hierarchy. If those whose faces fit get promoted to the top, the rest will follow suit and become 'Yes' men. They will give advice ministers want to hear to gain promotion rather than objective advice which may be unpopular. In her introductory statement to the note of guidance from the Head of the Civil Service on the duties and responsibilities of civil servants in relation to ministers, Mrs Thatcher expressly refuted this charge, stating, 'No competent Minister wants his civil servants to tailor their advice to what they think the Minister wants to hear' (HC Deb., vol. 68, col. 130, Written Answers, 26 February 1985). In this context the case of Sir Peter Kemp stands as a dire warning.

The biggest threat to the political neutrality of civil servants is when they are asked to perform party political functions. The line between governmental and political functions can be fine but there is a distinction. The use of a civil servant to leak the Solicitor-General's letter in the Westland affair can be said to be abusing the function of a civil servant, and Mrs Thatcher said she deeply regretted the method used for bringing the letter into the public domain (HC Deb., vol. 90, col. 653, 27 January 1986). Again Sir Bernard Ingham, Mrs Thatcher's press secretary, briefed newspaper correspondents on an unattributable basis, ie without allowing the source to be quoted, in a controversial and partisan manner which was more suitable for a party politician than a civil servant. More recently the Secretary of the First Division Association (the trade union of senior civil servants) has alleged in evidence to a House of Commons committee that civil servants were under increasing pressure from their superiors and ministers to engage in 'party political' work (HC 390-II, 1992–3, Q. 231 p. 61, Evidence to the Treasury and Civil Service Committee). Civil servants have also been involved in highly controversial party political issues such as checking on President-elect Bill Clinton's immigration records, the authorisation of the payment from public funds of the Chancellor of the Exchequer, Norman Lamont's, legal fees for evicting an undesirable tenant from his house and the Matrix Churchill affair involving the illegal export of arms-making equipment to Iraq. All these cases raised ethical questions about the standard of conduct of ministers or civil servants or both.

The position of civil servants who are asked to perform actions which they consider unethical is addressed in the revised note of guidance from the Head of the Civil Service on the duties and responsibilities of civil servants (HC Deb., vol. 123, col. 572, Written Answers, 2 December 1987). The original guidelines were drawn up following the Ponting case. Mr Ponting, a civil servant in the Ministry of Defence, leaked information to an MP because he felt that ministers were withholding information from a committee of the House of Commons. He was later acquitted for leaking confidential information contrary to the Official Secrets Act 1911. In such cases the guidelines provided for the matter to be reported to a senior officer and if appropriate to the Permanent Head of the Department. Whether this provision would have helped Mr Ponting is doubtful, it certainly did not help the civil servant who was asked to leak the Solicitor-General's letter in the Westland affair as her Head of Department was not available (HC 519, 1985–6, para. 174). In the last resort there is an appeal to the Head of the Civil Service. This has only been used once (HC 390-II, 1992–3, Q. 117). It is revealing that the Head of the Civil Service has dispensed civil servants from their duty of confidentiality and loyalty to the government, in compliance with their code of conduct, when giving evidence to the inquiry under Lord Justice Scott investigating the Matrix Churchill affair (HC 27i, 1993–4, Q. 1457). The revelations there about the conduct of ministers and civil servants have been startling.

This inquiry provides another illustration of the shield of anonymity being removed from civil servants. This also happened following the inquiry into the leak of the Solicitor-General's letter in the Westland affair, though in that case the civil servants were not allowed to defend themselves before the House of Commons committee investigating the issue because the Government insisted, in strict compliance with the convention of ministerial responsibility, that it is for ministers to investigate the conduct of civil servants and to decide which officials appear before these committees (HC 169, 1985–6, Q. 1064, Evidence to the Defence Committee).

However, civil servants are increasingly giving evidence in public to parliamentary committees about departmental policies and their implementation. This brings officials into the public eye and identifies them more openly with government policies. But they still appear on behalf of ministers to whom they are accountable for what they say and thus the figleaf of ministerial responsibility remains intact.

It has slipped badly as a result of recent developments which are moving in the direction of privatization of the civil service. Already two-thirds of the civil service has been reorganized into executive agencies which deliver public services, such as the Social Security Benefits Agency for the payment of social security benefits, the Driver and Vehicle licensing agency, the Meteorological Office, Her Majesty's Stationery Office, the Passport Office and up to 100 others. It is envisaged that only a small core of the civil service will eventually remain in conventional government departments. These agencies operate within the guidance laid down by framework documents which govern the policy and financial targets to be followed. This reorganization has had important repercussions for accountability. Though lip-service is paid to ministerial responsibility, it is the Chief Executive of the agency, who is increasingly likely to be recruited from outside the civil service, who is held to account before committees of the House of Commons and who cannot hide behind the minister in respect of matters within his delegated responsibility. Again, though parliamentary questions can still be addressed to ministers, those concerned with operational rather than policy matters are referred to the Chief Executive who writes to the MP. After much pressure from MPs these letters are now published in Hansard.

With the creation of executive agencies accountability has acquired a new meaning. Agencies are set performance as well as financial targets. They will be assessed by how far they achieve these targets and the pay of their Chief Executive on a fixed term contract can be affected accordingly. It is a business ethos rather than a public service culture which will predominate. The prevailing values will be economic and measurable rather than nonmaterial and unquantifiable, i.e. efficiency as against fairness. The Citizen's Charter which applies to the public services reinforces this trend by stressing performance indicators, complaints machinery and compensation for failing to meet targets. It sees the citizen as a customer of public services not as a member of a community whose needs have to be evaluated against those of others.

The same ethos is being further promoted by the pressure to contract-out services to the private sector wherever this is possible (Competing for Quality, Cm 1730, 1991). The running of certain prisons and the escort of prisoners by a private company, Group 4, are the fruits of this development. Its ultimate goal is full privatization such as the sale of the Property Services Agency.

Privatization and politicization are the Scylla and Charybdis threatening the civil service. Their menace will be greatly accelerated by the government's proposals for reorganization of the civil service published in July, 1994 (Cm 2627). It is not coincidental that they are both imports from the USA where the higher echelons of the civil service change with the President. This takes place, however, in the context of a written constitution based on the separation of the executive, legislative and judicial powers so that each can be a check on the other, in contrast to the sovereignty of Parliament which we must now examine in operation.

2

PARLIAMENT

THE HOUSE OF COMMONS

The House of Commons, which is the elected Chamber (the House of Lords will be discussed later), has a dual function: its role is both to sustain the government and to criticize it. This dichotomy runs through much of the work of the House of Commons and is the key to understanding the paradox that often Parliament is used as a synonym for the government because it acts as a rubber stamp; but it is also used in antithesis to the government, i.e. as a control mechanism. It would not be a solution to this conflict to say that the majority of the House fulfil one function and the opposition another, for the role of critic is performed by both sides of the House. Nor would it be correct to say that the role varies according to which task the House is performing, i.e. whether it is legislating or asking questions, for its critical and sustaining roles cut across these functions. It is when voting rather than expressing opinions that this dual role becomes most sharply focused, for MPs then have to make a clear decision as to whether to support the government or not. A vote of no confidence is, as we have seen, the ultimate weapon for defeating a government but almost certainly today at the cost of a dissolution of Parliament. Defeats on other issues illustrate the controlling function better because, unlike the bee's sting, they can be used more than once. Even these are likely to be rare and it is the daily give and take of debate and questioning which bring pressure to bear on the government, particularly under the constraints of time and coupled with the threat of possible

23

defeat, that wring concessions and compromises from the government, thus still making the House of Commons (and to a lesser extent the House of Lords) an important check on the elective dictatorship of the government.

That this check is by no means as powerful as it was in the last century is due to the growth of the party system which controls, first, who gets elected as an MP and then how he votes once he is an MP. We have seen how difficult it is under our electoral system to be elected unless one belongs to one of the two main parties; it is virtually impossible if one belongs to no party, though there have been some isolated exceptions. Once elected, the MP is the representative of his constituency which, as Edmund Burke made clear in his famous address to his Bristol constituents in 1774, does not constrain him to vote in accordance with their interests, i.e. he is not their delegate. In fact it is a breach of privilege of the House punishable as contempt for an MP's freedom of action to be fettered by an outside body. This has given rise to problems where MPs are sponsored by a trade union who contribute to his expenses or where they have other outside paid interests such as directorships or consultancies. Such interests are not banned, because the House would then become a body of professional politicians, but the House has resolved that they must be disclosed in debate and other proceedings and declared in a register of interests open to public inspection (HC Deb., vol. 874, col. 391, 22 May 1974 and vol. 227, col. 757 seq., 28 June 1993). These rules do not have the force of law but the House can use its own sanctions of suspension or expulsion to enforce them. Mr Browne, the MP for Winchester, was suspended for twenty days for failing to register an interest (HC Deb., vol 168, col. 973, 7 March 1990). These measures are designed to prevent conflict between an MP's private interests and his duty to represent the public interest. In reality, however, the biggest constraint on an MP's freedom of action comes from the party system.

Whipping

The mechanism for exerting pressure on an MP to toe the party line is the system of whipping. The Chief Whip and his assistant whips are members of the government whose task it is to ensure that MPs on the government side vote in accordance with the party whip which is a summons to vote graded according to importance, the three-line whip being the most peremptory. The opposition operates a similar system for its members. Withdrawal of the whip is the ultimate sanction for failure to vote with the party and may be the prelude to deselection of the MP by his constituency party. One Conservative MP had the whip temporarily withdrawn for failing to vote in the confidence debate on the Maastricht Treaty. A Tory MP has graphically described the pressures to which rebel or potentially rebellious MPs are subjected and the threats and cajolements which are brought to bear before a vote, such as that on the pay review for senior civil servants, military and judges, where there is a serious danger of a government defeat (*Guardian*, 2 August 1985). The ultimate deterrent of a General Election was hinted at, though probably not seriously. There are many lesser pressures which can be brought to bear, varying from not being allowed to go on a trip abroad with a parliamentary delegation, to not being considered for a ministerial post and being reported to the Constituency Chairman. 'One of the most brutal and controversial whipping operations for years' took place before the vote on the 'paving motion' for the Maastricht Bill (Baker, Gamble and Ludlam 1993, p. 158, supra p. 14). These pressure points epitomize the bondage of an MP to his party which reinforces the party loyalty which an MP naturally feels. They also distinguish today's MPs from their nineteenth-century forebears, who were not dependent on their seats for their livelihood, as many MPs are today.

Nevertheless, the pressure does not always work and some MPs are known as regular rebels. The crunch comes when the rebellion is large enough to inflict defeat on the government. The increase in such defeats in the 1970s (sixty-five defeats on the floor of the House of Commons between 1972 and 1979) has been noted (Norton, 1982, p. 112). Most of these were, however, inflicted on the minority Labour government between 1974 and 1979 and are therefore not typical for a majority government but more a foretaste of things to come under a hung Parliament. Mr. Major's government elected in 1992 with a majority of twenty-one has been considerably ham-strung by its small majority particularly on the Maastricht Bill because of the sizeable group of rebel Euro-sceptics. Not only was the government defeated on a specific amendment on 8 March 1993 (HC Deb., vol. 220, col. 715), which prolonged proceedings on the Bill by the need for a further stage of debate (the report stage) but the government also had to accept crucial amendments on the UK's opt-out from the social chapter of the Treaty to avoid defeat (HC Deb., vol. 223, col. 529, 22 April 1993 and ibid. vol. 224, col. 207, 5 May 1993). Also it could not use the usual mechanism for curtailing debate on a Bill, the guillotine (see below), because of the rebels on its backbenches and it had to rely on the opposition parties to move the closure when debating individual amendments. In the main votes on the principles of the Bill (the second and third readings) the government was not in danger because the Labour opposition abstained. The government has also been forced into making other concessions such as the reviewing of its pit-closure programme because of rebellion in its own ranks (HC Deb., vol. 212, col. 205, 19 October 1992).

However, a large majority can also be dangerous for a government, as Mr Pym remarked during the 1983 General Election, a warning which probably contributed to the loss of his Cabinet post. Mrs Thatcher's government, with a majority of 146, suffered defeats, most notably on the Shops Bill providing for Sunday opening (HC Deb., vol. 95, col. 694, 14 April 1986). The government tried to forestall defeat by offering a free vote on the later stages of the Bill. A free vote is traditionally used for non-party political issues of conscience (e.g. the abolition of capital punishment) but it can also be used to prevent defeat, as happened in the case of the Bill providing for direct elections to the European Assembly. In that case the free vote extended, as we saw, to members of the government (Chapter 1). Some free votes are less free than others. In the debate on the Water (Fluoridation) Bill members of the government were whipped (ibid., col. 689), and this also happened in the important debate on the procedure for Bills which will be considered shortly. Normally whipping applies not only on the floor of the House but when a Bill is considered in detail in committee. Defeats on amendments to the Bill are more frequent here because the majority of the government is smaller in proportion to the size of the committee. Such defeats can be reversed when the Bill returns to the floor of the House to be further amended. However, in the case of the Civil Aviation Bill in 1985 government rebels, who objected to the expansion of Stansted Airport, managed to get the committee stage halted altogether (Standing Committee F, 12 February 1985) and the Bill was abandoned, but this did not ultimately prevent the limited expansion of Stansted Airport.

It is arguable, therefore, that MPs hold the control of an elective dictatorship in their own hands. They have the vote and if they used it more frequently in accordance with their judgement rather than the party whip, the power of the government would be markedly curtailed. Undoubtedly MPs could exercise more independence and such a development would be accelerated in a hung Parliament, i.e. where no party had an overall majority. But it would be simplistic to underestimate the pressures of party loyalty and the party whips. The most potent antidote to the latter would be a system of voting in secret in the House of Commons instead of by walking through the lobbies. The potency of this system was shown in Israel, where it is used for the election of the President by MPs, when a Labour President was elected by a majority of MPs of the other parties in 1983. It is also revealing that the election of the party leader by Conservative MPs is by secret ballot. However valid in principle the arguments in favour of secret voting may be – and it has been made obligatory by the government for officers of trade unions (Trade Union Act 1984) – it is utopian to imagine that any government would concede the power this would confer on its backbenchers to defeat its policies with impunity except on a vote of confidence, where there would be the threat of dissolution. Such votes of confidence would probably then become more frequent.

The role of the opposition

Since such a utopian solution to the elective dictatorship is unlikely, the main burden of opposition to the government inevitably lies with the opposition. This has been institutionalized in a number of ways. Most significantly perhaps, the Leader of the Opposition is paid a salary as are a few other opposition officeholders (Ministerial and Other Salaries Act 1975), and in addition money is made available from public funds to opposition parties for their parliamentary work (HC Deb., vol. 888, col. 1869, 20 March 1975). Many would like to go further in strengthening advice for the opposition, to the extent of seconding civil servants to their staff (Wass, 1983). The rights of the opposition are enshrined in the procedure of the House of Commons. As we have seen, a motion of no confidence tabled by the opposition must be debated as soon as possible. At Prime Minister's question time the Leader of the Opposition is given priority over other MPs. In debate speakers alternate between government and opposition, and membership of committees is proportionate to the membership of the House. One of the problems encountered by the Liberal Democrats is that House of Commons procedure is adapted for the two-party system and does not easily accommodate a third party. This has led to a series of protests to procure recognition, most notably to obtain a share of those days expressly set aside for the opposition on which they may choose the subject for debate. They are now entitled to three out of the twenty 'opposition days' (see below).

Supply procedure

These 'opposition days' have an interesting history which is symptomatic of the relationship between the government and the House of Commons. Their origin lies in the days set aside for the discussion of public expenditure in the form of the annual estimates which, when embodied in the annual Appropriation Acts, legalize central government expenditure for that year. Originally there was no limit on the number of days set aside for discussion of the estimates. It was Balfour in 1896 who bargained a fixed number of days in return for a fixed date by which all the estimates had to be put to the vote. On these Supply days, as they came to be called, the opposition was given the right to choose the subject for debate. Increasingly, these days have been used by the opposition to discuss government policy rather than the details of government expenditure. There was rarely even a vote taken on whether an estimate should be granted to the government, and the Appropriation Acts, which legalized the expenditure, were passed purely formally without discussion except for the occasional protest at the farce that parliamentary control of expenditure had become. In 1982 the pretence of discussing expenditure on Supply days was dropped and they became called Opposition days. In addition three days were set aside for the discussion of expenditure, to be called Estimate days (HC Deb., vol. 28, col. 118, 19 July 1982). These days have been used for the discussion of reports of committees of the House which have been critical of particular areas of government expenditure. The debate takes place on a motion to approve a particular estimate which is then formally passed at the end of the debate. Very rarely has an amendment to reduce an estimate been put to the vote. The House of Commons has thus abdicated its function of discussing the details of government expenditure or even challenging them to a vote, preferring instead to use the allotted time to discuss issues of government policy selected by the opposition or one of its committees. This is partly the result of the intractability of the subject-matter and the inclination of politicians to discuss politics rather than economy of expenditure, but it also shows the dangers of a time-limit by which the House has to give its approval to government business, as it deprives the opposition of its strongest weapon which is time.

Legislative procedure

This has been the main topic of debate in relation to the procedure for approving legislation other than that authorizing government expenditure. The House has not abdicated its function to scrutinize the details of legislation including the annual Finance Act which authorizes taxation. Detailed discussion normally takes place not in the House as a whole, except in the case of Bills of constitutional importance such as the Maastricht Bill, but in standing committees, where the Bill is discussed clause by clause and line by line. It is here that concessions can be wrung from the government by applying pressure both from outside the House and within. A good illustration is the Police and Criminal Evidence Bill on which there were 105 sittings in committee (it had to be reintroduced after the General Election of 1983) and which ended as a very different Bill from the original one. Pressures were exerted by bodies like the Law Society, the BMA, the police and other professions outside the House, whilst the opposition and government backbenchers kept up a steady stream of amendments in the House. In many cases these were then adopted by the government in a modified form. The pressure is most potent when government backbenchers join forces with the opposition to make defeat possible. Even where this does not happen, the opposition have the weapon of time, because the government needs to get its legislative programme passed at the latest by the end of the parliamentary session (normally October) as it lapses otherwise. The government has a counter-weapon, the guillotine, a procedure which fixes a timetable for a Bill and automatically cuts off debate at the stated time. This is the equivalent procedure for Bills which applies automatically in the case of the estimates.

The use of the guillotine or timetabling of Bills goes to the heart of our democratic process, i.e. the relationship between government and Parliament, which for this purpose means the House of Commons. It is not coincidental that since 1979 when the Conservative government came to power there have been more guillotine motions than by all the previous governments this century. Whereas between 1945 and 1951 the Labour government passed its radical programme of nationalization and the creation of the welfare state through Parliament with the use of only three guillotines, the Conservative government used forty in the 1987–1992 Parliament alone, more than twice the number employed by the Labour government between 1974 and 1979 which did not have a majority most of the time. (HC Deb., vol. 205, col. 1103, 13 March 1992). This tells us much not only about the government but also about the opposition. It is indicative of the increasingly adversarial nature of party politics and the breakdown of consensus between the parties about the conduct of parliamentary business.

Not only has the number of guillotines increased in recent years but they have been imposed earlier. Guillotines used to be regarded as weapons of last resort to be imposed only after the opposition had filibustered to delay the Bill becoming law. They have been used increasingly to structure debate in committee so that discussion is not prolonged on the initial clauses and curtailed on the later ones after the guillotine has fallen (Ganz 1990, p. 496). The government is thus moving by stealth in the direction of the automatic timetabling of all controversial Bills which has been recommended by Procedure Committees of the House of Commons in 1985 and 1986 (HC 49, 1984–5 and HC 324, 1985–6) and reiterated in 1992 (HC 20, 1991–2). However, all these committees recommended that timetabling should be imposed by a specially appointed committee of MPs or by the standing committee to which the Bill is committed, not unilaterally by the government. There is a strong division of opinion on this issue within the House which cuts across party lines and no decision has yet been reached on this matter in the latest debate (HC Deb., vol. 211, col. 833 seq., 13 July 1992).

When the original recommendations of the Procedure Committee in 1985 were debated and put to the vote backbenchers but not members of the government were allowed a free vote and there arose the unusual spectacle of the government uniting with the opposition to defeat its own backbenchers in order to preserve the rights of the opposition (HC Deb., vol. 92, col. 1083 seq., 27 February 1986). In his speech the then Leader of the House, Mr Biffen, made what is still the most powerful defence of the status quo: 'All governments are tomorrow's possible opposition, and I think that my Right Hon. and Hon. Friends in their moments of supreme confidence, should consider, at least theoretically, how these proposals would bear upon the opposition. The Westminster political process is oblique and wide-ranging. It is like a seamless robe, which includes government legislation, and much else. At present, the opposition have opportunities for time and debate on legislation. If these are automatically extinguished, the opposition will be deprived of a pressure point which is often used to secure accommodation from the government, not merely on legislation, but on other points in the political process' (ibid., col. 1088). The Opposition Leader of the House, Mr Shore, congratulated Mr Biffen on his far-sighted and generous speech. Unfortunately time has eroded some of the force of this classic statement. As we saw above (p. 5), it can no longer be taken for granted that today's government is tomorrow's opposition. Secondly, some of the pressure points have been removed from the opposition by the use of guillotines earlier than previously. Here, as elsewhere in the constitution, it may no longer be possible to rely on self-restraint by the government and constitutional changes may be necessary to hold the government in check. It has been suggested by Graham Allen, a Labour MP, that the fundamental obstacle to the creation of a democracy in the UK is the lack of a separation of powers between government and Parliament and that Departmental Select Committees could play a central role in holding government to account (HC 19, 1989–90, p. xciii). It is to these committees that we must now turn.

Select committees

The model of parliamentary government which is implicit in the extract from Mr Biffen's speech is one of adversarial politics, where the government proposes and the opposition opposes and obtains modifications of the government's proposals by internal and external pressures. There is a totally different political model, namely the consensus model, where the aim is to reach agreement across the political divide by compromise and bargaining. The end result may be similar, as compromise may be achieved by either means, but the method used will be completely different.

Whether our adversarial politics is the result of our two-party system or not, the parliamentary procedures and the physical shape of the chamber of the House of Commons are geared to this system. Countries with multi-party politics have horseshoe-shaped chambers which symbolize the gradation of the political spectrum rather than its sharp division. If and when the two-party system breaks down in Britain and if proportional representation is adopted, coalition governments will have to be formed, which will involve moving towards the consensus model of politics. Even under our present adversarial system the alternative consensus model is followed in one area of House of Commons procedure, namely that of select committees. These committees, unlike the standing committees which consider legislation, do not debate but take evidence from witnesses by questions and answers and then normally make a report based on that evidence to the House as a whole. They have no powers except to make recommendations. They are constructed on the consensus model which is epitomized in their horseshoe-shaped seating arrangements.

The oldest select committee is the Public Accounts Committee which is the only mechanism by which the House of Commons examines the economy, efficiency and effectiveness of government expenditure. It has the assistance of expert auditors under the Comptroller and Auditor General whose reports to the committee form the basis of their examination of witnesses from government departments. Its chairman is by convention a senior opposition MP, to signify its impartiality and non-partisan nature. The same applies to the committee which scrutinizes delegated legislation (orders made by ministers under the authority of an Act of Parliament). The most important development of select committees came in 1979 when fourteen committees (there are now seventeen) were set up to scrutinize the work of each government department by examining its expenditure, administration and policy. The then Leader of the House said that they could constitute the most important parliamentary reform of the century (HC Deb., vol. 969, col. 35, 25 June 1979) which could alter the balance of power between the government and Parliament. Has this happened?

To emphasize the independence of the new committees the nomination of their members was entrusted not to the party whips but to another committee of the House (the Committee of Selection) who have evolved their own conventions, such as the exclusion of all frontbench spokesmen, which is intended to lessen partisanship. This does not, however, mean that the whips play no role in the appointment process. It is now openly stated that the whips are the channel through which names are put forward to the Committee of Selection on behalf of the two main parties but that the Committee makes the final selection (HC 19, 1989–90, para. 178). However, the interference of the whips was blatantly exposed after the 1992 election when a new rule was invented by the Committee of Selection banning government backbenchers who had served for three Parliaments on a select committee. This rule was designed to bar a particular back-bencher (Nicholas Winterton) from the Health Committee where he had been a thorn in the flesh of the government. It was condemned on both sides of the House which did not prevent the endorsement of the Committee's selection of MPs being carried by comfortable majorities (HC Deb., vol. 211, col. 913 seq., 13 July 1992). This highlights the innate weakness of the Departmental Committees *vis-à-vis* the government which under-mines every aspect of their work.

The Committees employ expert advisers, mostly on a part-time basis and on a very moderate scale. In the session 1988–9 there were under 100 staff in total servicing the committees (HC 19, 1989–90, para. 364). They also have power to order the atten-dance of witnesses and the production of documents. The limits of this power can be seen in the Westland Helicopter inquiry. As we have seen, the government refused to allow the civil servants involved in the leaking of the Solicitor-General's letter to give evidence to the Defence Committee inquiring into the affair. The Committee could have enforced attendance only through an order of the House of Commons where the government had a majority. It contented itself with reporting the matter to the House in its report on the Westland affair (HC 519, 1985–6, para. 231). In a debate on the report the government had a majority of 157 (HC Deb., vol. 103, col. 416, 29 October 1986).

The withholding of evidence from the Defence Committee inquiring into the Westland affair pales into insignificance beside what happened in relation to the inquiry of the Trade & Industry Committee into the export to Iraq of a supergun. The Committee's inquiry was obstructed by its inability to obtain evidence from the Customs and Excise department and from a Conservative MP, Sir Hal Miller (HC 86, 1991–2, para. 121 seq.). This is in sharp contrast to the powers of the court trying three company executives of Matrix Churchill Ltd prosecuted for supplying arms-making equipment to Iraq, which ordered documents to be disclosed, including ones relating to the security services, leading to the dropping of the prosecution. Also the Committee could not have obtained from civil servants the evidence which they gave to the Scott inquiry about confidential advice to Ministers (supra p. 20) because this is ruled out by the Memorandum of Guidance for Officials appearing before Select Committees (HC 19–II, 1989–90, pp. 206–231). These *causes célèbres* should not obscure the fact that much evidence has been made available to these committees, sometimes as a result of considerable pressure, which would not otherwise have seen the light of day, including some evidence made available to the committees conducting the Westland and Iraqi supergun inquiries. But no committee has yet taken a disagreement with the government about the production of evidence to the floor of the House. Though the government has promised to make time available for a debate if there was widespread concern in the House at the refusal to make evidence available to a committee, such a debate and the subsequent vote would put to the test whether MPs put loyalty to their committees above that to their party. The auguries from the debates on the Westland affair and the appointment of MPs to the committees (*supra*) are not happy. As Mr Tam Dalyell MP said recently, 'Party comes before Parliament in the House of Commons' (HC Deb., vol. 210, col. 810, 30 June 1992).

The inquiries conducted by the Defence and Trade and Industry Committees into the Westland and Iraqi supergun

affairs also illustrate one of the novel features of these committees. They can and do investigate instantaneously matters of
current concern in a way that the House of Commons cannot
do, namely by calling all those concerned, including ministers, to
be questioned in depth and then reporting their findings to the
House. The Education Committee was even able to settle an
industrial dispute threatening the Proms by giving both sides an
opportunity to state their case (HC 722, 1979–80). This function
of the committees to gather information from interested parties
and the government and make it available to the House and the
public has received most publicity, particularly when the hearing
is transmitted live on TV as was the case when the Chancellor of
the Exchequer, Mr Lamont, was being questioned on the events
of 'Black Wednesday' when the UK left the ERM (HC 201, 1992–3,
p. 1 seq.). The committees have contributed much to the cause of
open government.

This function, however, does not fundamentally change the
balance of power between government and Parliament. To do this
committees must carry weight with the goverment and Parliament. It is very difficult to evaluate the committees' impact on the
goverment, as they are one among many influences brought to
bear. Their recommendations are most likely to bear fruit where
the government is already thinking along the same lines, e.g. the
Home Affairs Committee's report on the law relating to public
order (HC 756, 1979–80). But they can also give an added impetus
to reforms, such as the same committee's report recommending
abolition of the 'Sus' law, which probably would not have
happened without the strong pressure of the committee (HC
744, 1979–80). If the committees can report before the government has crystallized its policy, they are more likely to have an
impact on government policy than by criticizing it *ex post facto*,
though the policy-making process is a continuing one and the
mere existence of the committees will make the government
sensitive to their anticipated reaction, knowing that they will
be called there to answer for their actions.

The impact of a committee's report is greater when it is
unanimous than if it splits along party lines but this did not

apply to the unanimous report of the Trade and Industry Committee on pit closures (HC 237, 1992–3) which was only partially accepted by the government in its White Paper 'The Prospects for Coal' (Cm 2235). There have been spectacular examples of such splits, notably the Foreign Affairs Committee's report on the events surrounding the sinking of the Argentine cruiser *Belgrano* (HC 11, 1984–5). However, the vast majority of reports have been unanimous and where there have been votes on parts of the report these have often cut across party lines. The striving for consensus could be said to be the hallmark of the committees. It is achieved partly by the choice of subjects for investigation. It was almost inevitable that an issue as emotive as the sinking of the *Belgrano* would give rise to fundamental disagreement. This has not, however, prevented the committees from dealing with highly controversial party political issues, such as the banning of trade unions at GCHQ, and reaching consensus on them (HC 238, 1983–4). In other cases a party split has been avoided by not making recommendations or by openly registering disagreement in the report. But in many cases subjects would not be chosen for investigation where a party split is a foregone conclusion. The achieving of consensus is made more difficult if the draft report by the chairman is prematurely leaked so that pressures can be brought to bear on members of the committee to toe the party line rather than make the compromises necessary to reach agreement, which is more likely to be reached behind closed doors. The decision of the House to treat such leaks seriously as breaches of parliamentary privilege, and to punish them accordingly, failed at the first attempt to apply it to a *Times* journalist who published a leaked report from the Environment Committee, because the person who leaked the report to him could not be found (HC Deb., vol. 98, col. 293, 20 May 1986). In an exceptional case involving the Health Committee the author of a leak of the chairman's draft report to the Department of Health was discovered to be a researcher employed by a Conservative MP on the committee, who had tabled a series of amendments to water down criticism of the government in the report (HC 614, 1990–91). The MP's resignation was welcomed by the committee (HC 34, 1991–2).

The consensus model which select committees follow is a source of weakness as well as strength. They exist as an oasis in an adversary system. This system limits both their functions and effectiveness. If they were given powers other than the power to make recommendations, the party whips would bring to bear the same pressures on members as they do in the House itself and the committees would split along party lines. The most fundamental weakness is the difficulty in transferring the consensus of the committee to the House itself. One of the novel features of the new committees is the extent to which they have tried to dovetail their reports with the work of the House. Though their reports are not often debated as such, in many more cases they are specially prepared in time for a debate on the subject. This was particularly true of the Treasury Committee's reports on public expenditure. But increasingly committees try to report on matters of public concern in time for a debate in the House. The new Estimate days are, as we have seen, used for debates on reports of the committees, though this still falls far short of a systematic examination of expenditure by the committees before approval by the House. Some committees have also made reports whilst a Bill is passing through Parliament in order to influence the legislative process. It is when such issues on which the committees have reported come to a vote in the House that the loyalty of members of the committees is put to the test. With some notable exceptions, e.g. in the debate on the 'Sus' report (HC Deb., vol. 985, col. 1763, 5 June 1980), members have voted with their party rather than their select committee and the consensus of the committee has not been transferred to the House itself.

The most blatant example of this occurred when MPs on the Trade and Industry Committee openly disagreed with each other about the interpretation of their unanimous report on pit closures when the issue was debated on the floor of the House. The government obtained approval for its policy by a comfortable majority, having placated by its modifications most of the rebels who had forced it into having a review of the closure programme

(HC Deb., vol. 222, col. 25, 29 March 1993). The same thing happened in the case of railway privatisation. The Transport Committee, chaired by a Conservative MP opposed to privatization, made an interim report in time for the Bill's second reading (HC 375, 1992–3) and a detailed final report containing dozens of recommendations in time for the Bill's report stage on the floor of the House (HC 246, 1992–3). The much heralded rebellion of Conservative MPs collapsed when the Transport Secretary made the minimum concessions needed to buy off the rebels, in particular over the continuation of concessionary railcards after privatisation (HC Deb. vol 225, col 758 seq., 25 May 1993). These recent examples illustrate the iron law of British politics that the only way in which concessions can be wrung from a government are by a threatened rebellion in its own ranks when it has a small majority. This cannot be altered by a reform of Departmental Committees on the lines suggested by Graham Allen MP. He recommended more independence for the committees through election by secret ballot, more staff, more power to send for witnesses and a bigger role in examining expenditure and legislation by having all Bills sent to them for examination (HC 19, 1991–2, p. xciii). These reforms could not solve the lack of a separation of powers between government and Parliament which he saw as the fundamental problem of our form of democracy. The committees have not altered the balance of power between the government and Parliament because they have not broken through the party political barrier. The crux of the matter was summed up by Mr Cunningham, a rebellious right-wing Labour MP who later defected to the SDP, when he said, 'In this place honourable Members often look for procedural prescriptions to ailments which are not procedural in nature but personal' (HC Deb., vol. 2, col. 1258, 10 April 1981). In other words the balance of power cannot be changed by improving procedures by select committees but by MPs using their votes.

THE HOUSE OF LORDS

The unelected part of Parliament, the House of Lords, is an anachronism. It consists of over a thousand peers, the majority of whom (over seven hundred and fifty) have inherited their titles and most of whom do not attend. The average daily attendance is over three hundred. Since the Life Peerages Act 1958 it has been possible to create life peers who, like the hereditary peers, are created by the Queen on the advice of the Prime Minister, who in some cases consults the opposition parties. There are now nearly four hundred life peers and they have transformed the party composition of the House of Lords. Though the peers taking the Conservative whip still form by far the largest group in the House of Lords, they no longer have an absolute majority over all the other peers, a considerable number of whom (about three hundred) sit on the cross-benches, which signifies their non-allegiance to any party. This group particularly includes former civil servants, the law lords who are created life peers under an Act of 1876 and those peers who have held high judicial office, e.g. Lord Denning. This change in party composition of the House of Lords through the creation of life peers and the non-attendance of most hereditary peers has profoundly affected the functioning of the House of Lords.

The House of Lords ceased to be the dominant part of Parliament as a result of the reform of the franchise in the nineteenth century, which made the House of Commons pre-eminent as the democratic chamber. But the House of Lords still had co-equal power over legislation, as all Bills had to be passed through the House of Lords as well as the House of Commons. Conventions developed about ultimately giving way to the elected House and there was always in the background the threat that the Prime Minister could ask the monarch to create sufficient peers in order to pass the legislation. It was this threat which enabled the great Reform Act 1832 to be passed. The threat was never put into practice (after 1712) but it played an important role in the constitutional crisis of 1909–11 when the House of Lords rejected the Liberal government's budget proposals. This led to a General Election which was won by the Liberal government. The King promised to create sufficient peers to force the House of Lords to assent to the curtailment of their powers provided that this met with the approval of the electorate. After a second General Election, which enabled the government to remain in power, the Parliament Act 1911 was passed which abolished the veto of the House of Lords for most Bills but not one which extended the life of Parliament beyond five years. Instead, they were able to delay Bills for up to two years which was cut down to one year in 1949. Again this power is more of a threat than a reality. The 1911 Act was only used three times to pass an Act, one of which was the Parliament Act 1949. One Act, the War Crimes Act 1991, has been passed without the consent of the House of Lords under the 1949 Act and the House of Lords used its delaying power for a year on a Trade Union Bill in 1975 and only allowed it to pass when the approval of the Lords was no longer necessary for it to become law. It is not, therefore, the use of the delaying power which is important, but its existence in the background still enables the House of Lords to wield considerable power over the content of government legislation. The exercise of this power operates under different constraints depending on whether a Labour or Conservative government is in office.

The problem of the House of Lords whichever government is in power is that it is unelected. This problem is accentuated when a Labour government is in office because of the in-built Conservative majority in the House of Lords, even though this is no longer absolute. Therefore, if the House of Lords uses its delaying power against a Labour government it will be accused of acting party-politically and obstructing the will of the people as expressed through the elected government. In retaliation the Lords will be threatened with abolition or at best reform. To cope with this dilemma conventions were evolved after the Second World War when a Labour government was elected for the first time with a large majority. The House of Lords would not use its delaying power for a Bill for which the government had a mandate, i.e. a proposal which was contained in the manifesto of the party which won the election. They would use this power only for a matter of great constitutional and national importance, to enable the government to think again and to allow public opinion to be mobilized. This convention was broken in 1976 when the House of Lords refused to pass the Aircraft and Shipbuilding Industries Bill which provided for the nationalization of those industries and which had been promised in the Labour party manifesto. Lord Carrington, who was then the Leader of the Opposition in the House of Lords, justified the action by reference to the Parliament Act itself. He said that it was for a situation such as this that the Act was devised, that unless the House of Lords had some power it would be useless and that the government was a minority one (HL Deb., vol. 377, col. 1678, 22 November 1976). In the end the Bill became law without the ship-repairing industry being included, in accordance with the wishes of the House of Lords. Apart from delaying the Trade Union Bill and emasculating the Aircraft and Shipbuilding Bill, the House of Lords defeated the Labour government 355 times between 1974 and 1979 (Shell, 1985). Such defeats may be irreversible when the Bill returns to the House of Commons if the government is in a minority or only has a small majority or needs to pass the Bill by a certain date. It was the experience of the Labour government between 1974 and 1979 which made the Labour Party Conference in 1977 vote for abolition of the House of Lords, though this was not included in the 1979 manifesto by Mr Callaghan. The Labour party is now in favour of an elected second chamber.

The position of the House of Lords when a Conservative government is in office is very different. If it uses its power to defeat the government it cannot be accused of acting party-politically because of the Conservative majority there, though it can be accused of acting undemocratically if it votes against a manifesto commitment. On the other hand a Conservative government cannot in practice use the threat of abolition if the Lords defy the government. In practice a Conservative government may have to accept more defeats by the House of Lords than a Labour government. Until recently, however, such defeats have been rare. Mr Heath's government was defeated only 26 times but from 1979 to 1992 the Thatcher/Major governments have been defeated about 200 times (*Observer*, 6 June 1992). These figures are impressive but they cannot be compared with those inflicted on the Labour government of 1974–9. The most important defeat came over the Bill to abolish elections for the GLC and the other metropolitan counties preparatory to the abolition of those local authorities. By convention the House of Lords does not vote against the second reading (the first debate on the principle of a Bill) where there is a manifesto commitment to which the Bill gives effect. However, at the next stage a fundamental amendment was carried to postpone implementation of the Act, because it would have allowed interim bodies with a different party political composition to take over the work of the existing councils before they had been legally abolished (HL Deb., vol. 453, col. 1069, 28 June 1984). This was considered unconstitutional by speakers in the House of Lords. The paradox lay in the unelected House defeating the elected House for acting undemocratically. The House of Lords was in fact performing the precise constitutional function which is the main justification for its existence. They were on a matter of great constitutional importance using their powers to make the government think again, a power which they alone could in these circumstances perform since the government had a majority of 146 in the House of Commons. With supreme irony the House of Lords, with Lord Hailsham, as Lord Chancellor, presiding on the Woolsack, was curbing the elective dictatorship to the delight of Ken Livingstone, the Chairman of the GLC, whose party was in favour of abolition of the Lords.

In retrospect this embarrassing defeat of the government over the 'Paving' Bill, as it came to be known, was the exception rather than the norm. On other highly controversial issues, where there had been unsuccessful rebellions by Conservative MPs in the Commons, such as the community charge (poll tax) and the imposition of charges for eye-tests, the much heralded defeats in the House of Lords did not materialize nor did it on the enactment of the Maastricht Treaty. Instead the government called on its supporters among the hereditary peers who rarely attend (the backwoodsmen) to defeat the rebels in its own ranks and opposition from the cross-benchers. Also it is not enough for the House of Lords merely to defeat the government, what matters is whether the defeat is accepted. On this there are no firm statistics because, as was pointed out in a recent debate, an amendment may be partially accepted (HL Deb., vol. 545, col. 1808, 19 May 1993). There is anecdotal evidence and some figures (Shell, 1992, p.157–8) to show that more often than not the Conservative governments since 1979 have accepted defeats in the House of Lords. Sometimes the government is forced into acceptance by lack of time if the defeat is inflicted towards the end of a Parliament, as happened on two Education Bills just before the General Election in April 1992. The same problem can arise at the end of a session of Parliament, which puts an end to all Bills which have not completed their passage through Parliament. If there is disagreement on an amendment there may develop a game of poker between the two Houses, each one having to guess whether insistence on its point of view will lead the other to accept defeat or wreck the Bill. There have been some interesting cliff-hangers, especially over the abolition of the mandatory life sentence for murder, which the Lords wanted to include in the Criminal Justice Bill 1991. Here the Lords climbed down as they did over railway privatization in 1993, but if the government give way they may reverse the defeat by subsequent legislation.

Where disagreement between the two Houses cannot be resolved, the Bill can still become law by use of the Parliament Acts. This happened for the first time under a Conservative government in the case of the War Crimes Bill 1991, which uniquely became law under the Parliament Act 1949. This Bill, which provided for the prosecution of war crimes committed in Germany or German-occupied territory during the Second World War by persons who later became British citizens, was a government Bill but not one contained in the manifesto. It was passed by a free vote through all its stages in the House of Commons. This was used as the justification by peers for breaking the convention and voting against the second reading of the Bill. The House of Commons then resorted to the Parliament Act 1949 and passed the Bill a second time a year later on a free vote.

It was rejected for a second time by the House of Lords with a much smaller majority than on the first occasion but this was an empty gesture, as its becoming law by virtue of the Parliament Acts was by then a foregone conclusion. The propriety of using the Parliament Acts for a Bill which was not party-political and was passed on a free vote in the House of Commons was hotly debated in both Houses. Those who opposed the use of the Parliament Acts thought they should only be invoked to prevent the opposition in the House of Commons using its majority in the House of Lords to frustrate the will of the elected government. Those in favour of resort to the Parliament Acts took the broader view that the unelected House had no right to frustrate the wishes of the elected representatives of the people which had been expressed on a free vote (Ganz, 1992).

The controversy over the War Crimes Act highlighted the paradox that the anachronistic and unelected House of Lords has the constitutional function to act as a check on the elected House. The Parliament Act 1911 recognizes this explicitly in exempting a Bill to extend the life of Parliament from its provisions. Even its worst enemies, like Mr Benn, recognize that if the House of Lords were abolished this constitutional gap would have to be filled. Other mechanisms would also have to be found for revising Bills that have passed through the Commons especially as so much legislation is introduced in haste without having been properly thought out. The proposals for reform of the composition of the House of Lords are all aimed at removing the anomaly of an unelected House, where one party has an in-built majority, acting as a revising chamber for legislation and ultimately as a constitutional safeguard. No solution has so far been found acceptable. The proposals of the Labour government in 1968 (Cmnd 3799) came nearest to being implemented but the Bill embodying them was torpedoed in the House of Commons through delaying tactics by an unlikely alliance of abolitionists, led by Michael Foot, and traditionalists, who wanted to keep the status quo, led by Enoch Powell. The proposals would have eliminated the anachronistic element by depriving most hereditary peers of the power to vote whilst allowing them to continue to sit in the House and speak. They would also have abolished the permanent Conservative majority through the creation by the government of the day of sufficient peers to give them a majority over all other parties but not over the whole House including the cross-benchers, who take no party whip. The cross-benchers would, therefore, have held the balance of power, though they rarely act as a cohesive force. The proposals would have increased the patronage in the gift of the Prime Minister and still have given power (though slightly reduced) to delay legislation to an unelected House. An elected House of Lords, which has been suggested by Lord Hailsham (1976) as well as by the Liberal Democrats and now the Labour party could become a rival to the House of Commons and was rejected in 1968 on those grounds. Its powers will, therefore, have to be carefully delimited and reform will have to wait until there is a change of government. In the meanwhile the present anachronistic House will paradoxically continue to be 'effectively the only place in which the legislature can curb the power of the executive.' (HL Deb., vol. 545, col. 1804, 19 May 1993)

3

ALLOCATION AND METHODS OF DECISION-MAKING

PREROGATIVE POWERS

All decision-making powers of public authorities derive from Parliament with the exception of those derived from the prerogative. These are the residual powers of the Crown which derive from the common law. They include such important powers as declaring war, making treaties, dispatching the armed forces, e.g. sending the Task Force to the Falklands and even requisitioning merchant ships, including the *QE 2*, during the Falklands conflict (Requisitioning of Ships Order 1982). Because power derives from the prerogative the government does not need the authority of Parliament for the exercise of these powers, though in practice Parliament will be informed in such important cases, as happened in the famous debate on Saturday, 3 April 1982 (HC Deb., vol. 21, col. 633) before the Task Force was dispatched to the Falklands. In the case of the Gulf War Parliament was recalled during the summer recess on 6 September 1990 (HC Deb., vol. 177, col. 734) to discuss the crisis after some British troops had already been dispatched. Another debate was held on 15 January 1991 (HC Deb., vol. 183, col. 734), the day on which the deadline for Iraq to comply with the UN resolution expired and before British troops went into action. Similarly, the instruction given by the Prime Minister prohibiting civil servants at the Government Communications Headquarters (GCHQ) from being members of a trade union, another illustration of a prerogative power, was announced to Parliament but only after it had been given, presumably for reasons of national security (HC Deb., vol. 52, col. 917, 25 January 1984).

Nothing can illustrate better the enormous difference both legálly and politically between the exercise of power by the government under the prerogative instead of statute than the controversy surrounding ratification of the Treaty on European Union signed at Maastricht. The power of the government to agree and ratify international treaties is derived from the prerogative. The consent of Parliament is only required for those parts of the Treaty which need to be incorporated into UK law. This applied only to certain parts of the Maastricht Treaty. Parliament cannot amend a treaty, it can only refuse to enact it into domestic law. The critics of the Maastricht Treaty had to find ways to circumnavigate this rule by their amendments to the Bill (the European Communities (Amendment) Bill 1993). The most controversial amendment concerned the Social Chapter, an agreement to implement the Social Charter concerned with the conditions of workers, which the UK had opted out of. The amendment to exclude the opt-out from the Bill was first said by the government to have the effect, if passed, of wrecking the treaty. After taking legal advice from the Attorney-General the government announced that it would have no legal effect and would not prevent ratification of the treaty, as it was, including the opt-out (HC Deb., vol. 219, col. 27 seq., 15 February 1993). They later accepted the amendment without a vote to deprive their opponents of an 'entirely synthetic victory' (HC Deb., vol. 224, col. 207, 5 May 1993). The constitutional enormity of this stance was expressed succinctly by the opposition spokesman: 'the Government would use the royal prerogative to ignore Parliament' (HC Deb., vol. 219, col. 29, 15 February 1993). However, the government's view was upheld by the court when it dismissed the action to prevent ratification of the Treaty brought by Lord Rees-Mogg (*R v. Foreign Secretary ex parte Rees-Mogg*, 1994).

Meanwhile the opposition had devised another mechanism to force the government's hand on the Social Chapter. They put forward a new clause which would prevent the Act coming into force until each House of Parliament had come to a Resolution on a motion considering the adoption of the Social Chapter. This clause, too, was finally accepted by the government without a vote, thereby pre-empting defeat (HC Deb., vol. 223, col. 529 seq., 22 April 1993). This was the time-bomb which exploded on 22 July 1993 (HC Deb., vol. 229, col. 608) when the House of Commons had a tied vote, later corrected to a majority of one (ibid., col. 623), against an opposition amendment to prevent the government ratifying the Treaty until it had notified its intention to adopt the Social Chapter. But it then defeated by 8 votes the government motion to take note of the government's policy on opting-out of the Social Chapter, with 23 Conservative rebels voting against the government. This was immediately followed the next day by a motion which made the government's opt-out from the Social Chapter an issue of confidence, which the government won comfortably by 40 votes (HC Deb., vol. 229, col. 721, 23 July 1993). Instead of using the blunderbuss of the royal prerogative to ratify the Treaty with the opt-out against the wishes of the House of Commons, it had to use the nuclear deterrent of a confidence motion. The effect of the fall-out from the explosion is incalculable.

DELEGATED LEGISLATION

Parliament can make only a limited number of decisions in the form of legislation. Acts of Parliament should lay down the principles but their detailed implementation has to be delegated to ministers. The Act will give power to a minister to make regulations, called statutory instruments, for this purpose, i.e. rules drafted in his Department which the Act may provide shall be laid before Parliament either for approval or for annulment. In the former case the government has to provide time to debate the instruments for at least one and a half hours, though in some important cases more time has been allowed for debate. In the case of annulment MPs, normally from the opposition, have to put down a prayer and debates are held after 10 p.m. and are cut off at 11.30 p.m., when the vote takes place, which, if the government has a majority, will normally be a foregone conclusion. Of the over three statutory instruments which are now made every year the vast majority are not subject to parliamentary approval and only a small number of prayers are debated late at night. There is thus little opportunity to debate statutory instruments on the floor of the House and no possibility of amending them unless a minister can be persuaded to withdraw the instrument and bring it back in a different form. It is now possible for statutory instruments to be debated in a standing committee but they have to return to the House to be approved or annulled there. The two standing committees which have been set up for the consideration of proposals for European Community legislation made by the institutions of the European Community can question a minister before debating the document.

The lack of parliamentary scrutiny is inherent in the use of statutory instruments, as they are intended to save parliamentary time. So long as they deal with the nuts and bolts of legislation this is acceptable. There is, however, a growing tendency to use statutory instruments for matters of policy and principle which should be embodied in the Act itself. Thus the Education (Student Loans) Act 1990 is effectively nothing more than an authorization for the Secretary of State for Education to make arrangements for enabling students to receive loans towards their maintenance whilst attending courses of higher education. Such framework or skeleton Acts which may contain over 100 regulation-making powers, as in the Child Support Act 1991, are becoming increasingly common. While such Acts may be acceptable in time of war or emergency such as the Emergency Powers (Defence) Act 1939, they fundamentally alter the balance of power between Parliament and the executive, particularly when the subordinate legislation is subject to little or sometimes no parliamentary oversight. The courts have even been moved to comment unfavourably on such blanket delegation of power in the case of social security legislation (*R. v. Secretary of State for Social Security ex parte Stitt, Guardian*, 10 July 1990). The most criticized form of delegation is that which gives ministers powers by regulation to amend an Act of Parliament, called Henry VIII clauses. All these developments have given rise to much concern in Parliament and in particular in the House of Lords, which has resulted in the setting up there of a new committee on an experimental basis. The Delegated Powers Scrutiny Committee scrutinises every government Bill as to whether it inappropriately delegates legislative power or provides for an inappropriate degree of parliamentary scrutiny and reports to the Lords before the Committee stage. Skeleton Bills and Henry VIII clauses are prime targets for report. The Committee made a damning report on part of the Education Bill 1994 dealing with student unions because it was a 'skeleton bill' and interfered with the freedom of association of students (HL 11, 1993–4). These provisions were later dropped from the Bill (HL Deb., vol. 552, col. 57, Written Answers, 24 February 1994). The most far-reaching proposals for delegated legislation are contained in the Deregulation and Contracting Out Bill 1994 which would allow a minister to make an order to amend or repeal primary legislation which imposes an unnecessary burden on a trade or business, provided necessary protection in the original Act of Parliament is not removed. The Procedure Committee of the House of Commons has made recommendations for a new Committee to be appointed with power to scrutinise and even reject such orders (HC 238, 1993–4). The latter recommendation has not been accepted by the government (HC 404, 1993–4). The House of Lords failed to act as guardian of the constitution in the case of this Bill which confers powers unprecedented in peacetime.

Whilst at one end of the spectrum statutory instruments are being used for provisions which should be contained in Acts of Parliament, at the other end statutory instruments are being replaced by codes of practice, codes of conduct, guidelines, circulars and a miscellany of rules which have been given the title of 'quasi-legislation'. Unlike statutory instruments, this material has varying degrees of legal force. Its legal effect will depend on the Act under which it is made. The Highway Code is probably the first illustration of this development. Breach of the code is not a criminal offence but it can be taken into account in any criminal or civil proceedings (Transport Act 1988, section 38). This provision has been used in an increasing number of areas including health and safety at work, industrial relations, race relations, animal welfare and control of pollution. The main reason for using codes with limited legal effect in preference to legal regulations was a preference for the voluntary approach. In these situations it was thought that persuasion would be more effective than compulsion and codes would be more advisory and persuasive than legal regulation. They also have the practical advantage of not having to be couched in precise legal language and they can also be more flexible. However, their flexibility will depend very much on the procedural safeguards which regulate their making and approval. Here there are a plethora of different provisions in the parent Acts but certain standard control mechanisms recur in many statutes. There is often provision for consultation with affected interests, parliamentary approval or the opportunity for annulment and publication. The difficulty of locating this material, because publication takes such diverse forms, has been one of the main criticisms of these mechanisms for laying down rules from the beginning of this development.

Quasi-legislation is used to regulate the conduct not only of private individuals but also of public authorities. The codes of practice made under the Police and Criminal Evidence Act 1984 may be regarded as a prototype. These lay down the way in which the police should exercise their functions under the Act in much more detail than the Act itself. Breach of the codes makes the police liable to disciplinary proceedings but does not render them liable to criminal or civil proceedings, though it must be taken into account in such proceedings where relevant (section 67). Similar provisions are now contained in statutes concerned with local government and provide for codes directed to local authorities. The novelty lies in embodying in Acts of Parliament provisions for such codes of guidance to local authorities. Until recently such guidance, usually contained in circulars from a government department to local authorities, was provided without any statutory provisions. This is still the position in most cases. The circulars are often a mixture of explanation and advice and they have been used in some cases as a substitute for legislation because the government preferred persuasion to legal regulation of local authorities. Thus circulars were used by the Labour government in 1965 to implement its policy for comprehensive education, and legislation was only used as a last resort to bring a few recalcitrant authorities to heel in 1976.

Quasi-legislation can be abused when it is used to by-pass Parliament by putting politically controversial provisions in a code of practice instead of an Act of Parliament. This happened with the code on picketing, made under the Employment Act 1980, which limited the number of pickets to six, a figure which was not included in the Act, but has become law by the back door, because the code has to be taken into account by the courts. Where there is consensus on a code it can be more effective than law in ensuring compliance, as well as having practical advantages, but the procedures for the making, publication and parliamentary scrutiny of codes need to be systematized.

INTERPRETATION AND APPLICATION OF LEGISLATION AND DELEGATED LEGISLATION

Tribunals

Rules, whether laid down in an Act or in regulations made under an Act, have to be interpreted and applied to individual cases. Interpretation of statutes and statutory instruments is a matter for the courts but Acts of Parliament may entrust this function to other bodies, though, as we shall see, these will themselves be subject to the supervision of the courts. In an increasing number of areas tribunals have been preferred to courts as decision-making bodies. There are some two thousand tribunals covering such diverse areas as social security, immigration, employment, taxation, and the national health service. The reasons for preferring tribunals to courts are both practical and ideological.

Tribunals do not consist of lawyers, though increasingly the chairman is a lawyer appointed by the Lord Chancellor. The other members may be representatives of interest groups, e.g. employers or employees in the case of industrial tribunals, or they may have a particular expertise, e.g. doctors in the case of mental health tribunals. When some of the tribunals were first set up after 1945 it was made explicit by the government that the courts were not trusted to decide disputes in certain areas of social policy such as national insurance, rent and the national health service. Later criticism centred on the members of tribunals being drawn from a narrow social spectrum and being unfamiliar with the problems of the people appearing before them, particularly in the case of supplementary benefit appeal tribunals. It has also been alleged that in certain cases tribunals have been used to give the appearance of impartiality to the implementation of controversial policies. This allegation has been made particularly against supplementary benefit appeal tribunals and immigration tribunals (Harlow and Rawlings, 1984, p.75 seq). The policies are embodied in the Acts and regulations or rules made under them, the tribunals can only interpret and apply them. If ministers do not approve of the interpretation in a particular case, it can always be reversed by changing the law. Ministers cannot interfere directly in individual cases but they have been known not to publicize unfavourable decisions so as to limit their impact, or to settle test cases in order to prevent an unfavourable decision. Tribunals were firmly categorized as part of the machinery for adjudication rather than administration by the Franks Committee which was asked to investigate the constitution and working of tribunals in 1957 (Cmnd 218). To achieve impartiality, which was one of its aims for tribunals, it recommended that members should be neither appointed nor dismissed by ministers. This was only partly implemented so that chairmen are usually appointed by the Lord Chancellor or from a panel of members appointed by him, and all members can normally be removed only by him. As most members hold office only for a limited period, this latter safeguard is not very significant.

The practical advantages of tribunals are procedural. In general they are cheaper, quicker and more informal than courts, though the variations between tribunals are as great as their differences from the courts. Some, like the Lands Tribunal, are indistinguishable from a court in all but name, whilst in a social security tribunal all the participants, including the members of the tribunal, may sit round a table. In between these extremes of formality, the members of an industrial tribunal may sit on a raised dais with the parties sitting at tables in front of them. Procedure varies accordingly from an almost informal conversation round the table to a full-scale hearing with the parties represented by lawyers and evidence on oath. Legal aid is not available for representation before almost all tribunals and many applicants, therefore, appear in person or may not appear at all in the case of social security tribunals. Some see the remedy for this in making legal aid or other representation more widely available, so that the parties are more evenly matched. Alternatively, it is possible to see the members of tribunals playing a more active role in the proceedings, as many do in practice, by asking questions and bringing out the salient issues. There is also evidence that applicants prefer to play a more active role in the proceedings rather than listening passively to their lawyer present their case (Bell, 1975, p. 16). Neither of these remedies affects the outcome of proceedings as much as specialist representation (Genn, 1993). If tribunals are too closely modelled on courts they lose the procedural advantages which were the main justification for their creation. On the other hand, they must be seen to be fair and independent from the government department concerned if they are to be trusted by the citizen.

Latterly there has been an increasing trend to substitute the principles of economy, efficiency and expedition for the ideals of openness, fairness and impartiality advocated by the Franks Committee. This has resulted in the provision of internal review procedures within a government department or agency instead of an appeal to an independent tribunal. The most striking example is the use of this procedure for refusals of lump sum benefits under the Social Fund to recipients of income support. Formerly an appeal lay to a tribunal in this type of case. This trend has been deplored by the Council on Tribunals which is the statutory watchdog overseeing the working of tribunals (HC 64, 1990–91).

Ministers

Ministers entrust to courts, tribunals or any other independent body those individual decisions which they do not wish to take themselves, though they usually reserve the power to lay down the policies to be applied by such bodies. The rationale behind such allocation is very varied and by no means consistent either between governments of different party political complexions or even between those of the same political colour. Thus the Labour opposition opposed giving wide discretionary powers to the Restrictive Practices Court to determine whether restrictive trade agreements were against the public interest. On the other hand a subsequent Labour government entrusted wide discretionary powers to immigration tribunals when determining immigration appeals, which was opposed by the then Conservative opposition. In contrast, governments of both parties have refused to entrust decisions about the provision of grants to assist industry to a court or tribunal, even where detailed criteria were laid down by statute, because they wished to reserve questions of interpretation to themselves. Again, governments of both parties may agree to give wide discretionary powers to an independent body so as to eliminate political considerations, e.g. the allocation of licences by the Independent Television Commission. When governments want to take into account their own policy in reaching a decision and do not want to entrust its interpretation to another body, they will reserve the decisions to themselves, though in practice only the most controversial cases will be decided by ministers personally. The rest will be decided by civil servants in the Department, the level at which the decision is made depending on its importance.

Where decisions are made by government departments in the name of the minister the procedure may be completely informal. This is the position with regard to grants to assist industry. These are negotiated between the applicant and officials in the Department who interpret the statutory provisions and internal guidelines which supplement them. A firm which may be disadvantaged by the granting of assistance to a rival concern has no opportunity to object. Governments have rejected all attempts by MPs to formalize these procedures by making the Department give reasons for its decision, though applicants are given guidance about the criteria that the

Department uses. Governments have insisted on retaining the maximum flexibility for these potentially politically sensitive decisions, refusing to be bound by any appeal mechanism or outside advisory body.

PUBLIC INQUIRIES

In marked contrast to this informal decision-making process for decisions which can involve the public expenditure of millions of pounds is the elaborate public inquiry procedure which is obligatory for a vast number of decisions varying from the appeal against a refusal of planning permission to the building of roads, airports and nuclear power stations. It is revealing that the same basic procedure is prescribed for such widely disparate decisions, whose only common feature is that they involve interference with private land and that their origin lies in the private Act of Parliament which at one time had to be passed before these rights could be taken away compulsorily. The procedure for passing such Acts, which were used for the building of the railways and canals involves a judicial-type hearing before a small committee in each House. This procedure gave rise to much controversy in the 1980s because it was used for some highly politically controversial Bills, in particular Bills to expand private ports to enable the importation of foreign coal which led to the closure of British pits. MPs also resented the use of private Bills to by-pass planning procedures, as happened in the case of the Lyndhurst Bypass Bill (HC 650, 1987-8). After a report from a Joint Committee of both Houses (HL 97, 1987-8) the Transport and Works Act 1992 provided that a minister could authorize railway and tramway schemes by statutory instruments after hearing objections at a public local inquiry. If he considers the scheme to be of national significance the approval of both Houses of Parliament is necessary before the proposal can proceed to a public inquiry. Thus Parliament has divested itself of more powers and delegated them to ministers but it has also recognized that the public local inquiry is a better mechanism for public participation than Parliament itself.

A public local inquiry is held before an inspector appointed by the minister who conducts the inquiry and reports to the minister. He, or in most cases his officials, then makes the decision, usually without any parliamentary involvement. The public inquiry procedure still performs its original function of protecting landowners in the run-of-the-mill appeal by an applicant against refusal of planning permission by a local authority. In most of these cases the power to make the decision is now vested in the inspector, which in practice means that they are made by a different type of official, as few decisions reach the minister himself. In most cases the applicant now opts for an informal written procedure but he has the statutory right to a full oral hearing. The Council on Tribunals fought a successful battle to prevent the removal or watering down of this right by the Planning and Compensation Act 1991 (Council on Tribunals Report for 1990–91). This proposal formed part of a package of provisions in the Act to streamline the planning system in the interests of efficiency. Again we see the pursuit of speed and economy at the expense of fairness.

At an inquiry the main protagonists are no longer just the local authority who refused permission and the applicant for such permission, but third parties, e.g. neighbours and those concerned with the wider environment who, though they have no legal rights, are allowed to state their views to the inquiry and whose representations may be taken into account. This has turned many such inquiries into contests between private landowners rather than resolving conflicts between the private and public interest, though the public interest is only an amalgam of private interests. A neighbourhood is merely a collection of neighbours. As has been said elsewhere, one man's property is another man's environment (Ganz, 1974, p. 55).

The judicialization of inquiries received a strong impetus from the Franks Committee (Cmnd 218, 1957) which was asked to investigate the procedure of inquiries as well as tribunals. It made many recommendations, which were mostly implemented, to make the procedure more like a court hearing than an administrative procedure designed to inform the minister. Reasons now have to be given for decisions and the inspector's report has to be published, and the minister cannot disagree with his findings except on matters of policy without giving the parties further opportunities to make representations or reopening the inquiry. As a result, inquiries have become more court-like with parties represented by lawyers, adopting courtroom techniques of cross-examination before an inspector whose judicial appearance Franks wanted enhanced by putting his appointment into the hands of the Lord Chancellor. This has not been implemented, except many years later in the case of motorway inquiries, but the natural corollary of these developments has been to turn the inspector into the judge who makes the decision in the case of most planning appeals which are not politically controversial. The controversial cases can always be called-in for decision by the minister and it is in these major inquiries into projects such as the building of a third London airport, or a new type of nuclear power station at Sizewell or, to a lesser extent, the building of motorways that most problems have been encountered in adapting the highly judicialized public inquiry procedure as a prelude to important political decisions.

By widening the terms of reference of the inquiry to investigate the need for the project, in addition to its siting at a particular place and by adding expert assessors to assist the inspector, who can commission his own research, the inquiry has been broadened into an investigation of major political and economic issues such as the desirability of nuclear power or airports policy. This examination takes place within the straitjacket of a court-like procedure with the major participants represented by high-powered lawyers. The inspector's report and recommendations are made to the minister and the ultimate decision in such important cases may well be made at Cabinet level. The inspector's recommendations, reached after years of investigation, may be overturned for purely political reasons, as happened to the recommendations of the Roskill Inquiry into the siting of the third London airport in 1971. Parliament has as a rule no legal role to play in these decisions, which it has conferred on ministers, but recently it has insisted on debating the issues before decisions are made. This has involved difficult contortions so as not to fall foul of the legal provisions relating to the handling of the inspector's report by the minister. All these difficulties epitomize the problem of reaching a political decision through a judicial procedure. A two-stage procedure has been recommended whereby the policy issues about the need for the project are investigated by a more inquisitorial type of procedure, preferably without lawyers, and only if approval is given for the project would there be a public inquiry into where it should be sited (Outer Circle Policy Unit, 1979). Unfortunately the multi-stage Roskill Inquiry, which lasted for two and a half years, has made governments wary of adopting such procedures.

In stark contrast to these public inquiry procedures for major projects is the use of the hybrid Bill procedure for authorizing the building of the Channel Tunnel. The same procedure is to be employed for the construction of the Channel Tunnel rail link. A hybrid Bill is a government Bill, which has a committee stage like a private Bill, where a small committee hears objectors who can show an interest affected by the Bill in accordance with strict criteria laid down by each House. The committee cannot question the principle of building the project which is decided when the Bill gets a second reading. The use of this procedure for authorizing the Channel Tunnel in 1986–7 was strongly criticized because it was much quicker and gave less scope for objections to be heard than a major public inquiry which may last for years. These criticisms echo those made by members of both Houses about private Bill procedure and illustrate how far we have moved in this area from a representative to a participatory democracy, where individual citizens and pressure groups expect to be consulted.

CONSULTATION AND OPEN GOVERNMENT

The consultation of affected interest groups before decisions are made by the government is well established in certain areas but is by no means universal. Acts of Parliament are normally preceded by consultation with those affected, though this may be very cursory and without any noticeable effect (Making the Law, Hansard Society, 1992, Chapter 3). Bills are often preceded by consultation papers, followed by White Papers setting out the government's proposals on which further consultation takes place before the Bill is drafted. Both types of document may also be debated in Parliament. Similar procedures may be used for delegated legislation. Some town planning regulations have been preceded by consultation papers and the Highway Code has been through such a consultation stage. Consultation on statutory instruments which may go through many drafts is now the norm, though this is rarely provided for by statute. In the case of statutory codes of practice there is frequently a duty to consult affected interests embodied in the statute. Even non-statutory circulars have been subjected to intensive consultation, such as the Department of Environment circular dealing with green belts round built-up areas. There have also been startling examples of the lack of consultation, such as the instruction by Mrs Thatcher prohibiting employees at the secret Government Communications Headquarters from being members of trade unions, which the courts would have held to be unlawful but for the considerations of national security involved (*Council of Civil Service Unions v. Minister for the Civil Service*, 1984). It has even been held by the Court of Appeal that a non-statutory circular on immigration by the Home Secretary could not be changed without giving an applicant in receipt of the circular an opportunity to make representations (*R. v. Home Secretary ex parte Asif Khan*, 1984). But it is doubtful whether this case can be applied generally to changes of policy by which individuals are deleteriously affected. In a case where there were statutory provisions for consultation of those affected by the regulations, the court held that it was unfair in the circumstances not to show them the advice of independent experts on which the regulations were based and quashed the regulations (*R. v Health Secretary, ex parte U.S. Tobacco*, 1991).

Consultation may be institutionalized by making it obligatory to consult an advisory body, as is the case with social security regulations. It is also now becoming more common for the departmental select committees to consider regulations, codes of practice and even circulars before they are debated in the

House of Commons or reach their final form. Such committees also examine policy statements from the government which may be contained in White Papers and preceded by consultation papers. Both consultation papers and White Papers may invite further comments from the public, though this is more usual with the former than the latter. Draft policy statements may also be used for this purpose. There is enormous variation in the extent to which the policy-making process by the government is open to public debate. The review of the supplementary benefits scheme by a team of officials in the Department of Health and Social Security in 1978 (Social Assistance) was not only published but members of the team answered questions at meetings throughout the country. This was a rather exceptional exercise in open government. Though there was a general directive by the Head of the Civil Service in 1978 to publish factual background material to policy studies unless ministers decided otherwise (HC Deb., vol. 942, col. 691, Written Answers, 26 January 1978), a later Head of the Civil Service stated that the reasons for deciding against publication might often be nothing more weighty than political embarrassment (Wass, 1983). The degree of political embarrassment which can be caused by exposing the policy-making process to public view was nowhere better illustrated than during the Westland affair when Cabinet meetings and confidential departmental meetings were openly discussed in Parliament and the media. These revelations pale into insignificance beside those made to the Scott inquiry into the Matrix Churhill Affair. The leaking of confidential letters written by ministers and civil servants is now commonplace.

These frequent leaks can be seen as symptoms of a system of closed government. Mr Major's government has taken some steps towards more openness such as the publication of the committees of the Cabinet (HC Deb., vol. 208, col. 110, Written Answers, 19 May 1992) and the publication of a Memorandum of Guidance, 'Questions of Procedure for Ministers' (Cabinet Office, 1992), which was hitherto secret. He has even appointed a minister with responsibility for open government as well as the Citizen's Charter. The latter provides for the publication of much information such as performance targets and league tables of performance. All this falls far short of a legal right for the citizen to obtain government documents subject to specific exceptions. This has so far been resisted by the government. The Right to Know Bill introduced by a Labour MP with all party support in 1993 would have provided for such a right of access to documents of public authorities with exceptions for documents causing significant damage to defence, law enforcement, the economy, the security services or international relations. It would have exempted policy advice from civil servants but not factual information on which it is based. It would also have allowed exempt information to be published where it was in the public interest to disclose abuse of authority, negligence or injustice.

The Bill would also have given a public interest defence to those charged under the Official Secrets Act where there had been abuse of authority or other misconduct, which could cover circumstances similar to those of Mr Ponting who leaked information about the sinking of the *Belgrano*. The notoriously wide Section 2 of the Official Secrets Act 1911 under which he was prosecuted has been repealed by the Official Secrets Act 1989 and replaced with specific categories of information which it is a criminal offence for a Crown servant to disclose without lawful authority. The Act covers information damaging to the security services, defence, international relations and criminal investigation, as well as imposing a life-long duty of confidentiality on members of the security services. This enshrines in criminal law the duty which the House of Lords affirmed as protected by the civil law of breach of confidence in the *Spycatcher* case (*AG v. Guardian Newspapers*, 1988) arising out of the publication of the memoirs of a former member of the security service.

The Right to Know Bill completed its committee stage with the help of Conservative MPs. It was blocked at the report stage (HC Deb., vol. 204, col. 1283, 2 July 1993) and the government has made its own proposals for more openness in a White Paper on Open Government (Cm 2290). In 1994, the government issued a Code of Practice committing government departments to publishing facts and analyses of facts considered relevant in framing major policy proposals when the decisions are announced, giving reasons for administrative decisions and meeting reasonable requests for information relating to policies, actions and decisions of departments. There are the usual exemptions for information which would harm national security, defence, law enforcement, the economy, personal privacy and confidentiality and for internal policy advice. The Code will be policed by the Parliamentary Commissioner for Administration (Ombudsman) to whom complaints can be made if information is withheld in breach of the Code. He will be able to recommend disclosure and his recommendations have almost always been accepted (below p. 94).

The government explicitly rejected the courts or a tribunal as enforcement mechanisms on the grounds that this would be too rigid and would delegate political decisions to appointed judges. In other words ministers were not prepared to give up having the last word in this sensitive area. This is the fundamental difference between a statutory 'right to know' as contained in the Bill and the Code of Practice. The Code, therefore, represents a rather half-hearted commitment to government in the sunshine, to borrow the American phrase, which provides the best antiseptic against corruption. Democracy has been aptly defined as government by explanation.

Quangos and nationalized industries

Where governments want to take decisions out of the political arena but do not want to entrust them to the courts or tribunals, they can allocate them to a public body set up for this purpose. These bodies can be loosely described as quasi-autonomous non-governmental organizations (quangos). They can be used for very different purposes and set up by governments of opposite political persuasions. Some exist with all-party agreement, others are subject to acute political controversy. At some times they are very much in fashion, at other times severely under attack, and these fluctuations cut across party lines. The Labour government after 1945 set up public corporations to run the nationalized industries or non-commercial services such as the New Town Development Corporations. Mr Heath's Conservative government in 1970 followed the advice of the Fulton Committee on the Civil Service (Cmnd 3638, 1968) to hive off activities from the civil service for reasons of managerial efficiency. Mrs Thatcher has waged war on quangos as symbols of patronage, bureaucracy and public expenditure but this did not prevent her from creating new ones where she thought it necessary, such as the urban development corporations for London's Docklands and other inner city areas and the boards which have taken over some of the functions of the GLC and Metropolitan County Councils which were abolished by the Local Government Act 1985. Some bodies like the BBC, the Independent Television Commission and the Arts Council have been generally recognized as useful buffers protecting the area in question from direct political interference. On the other hand, the National Enterprise Board and its predecessor, the Industrial Reorganization Corporation, set up by Labour governments to give assistance to industry, were each axed by the succeeding Conservative governments because they were not politically acceptable. Quangos are neither good nor bad, the basic question is to what extent it is desirable that decisions should be distanced from political considerations and be taken by experts applying commercial, artistic or professional criteria. The corollary of independence from political control is lack of democratic accountability, though there may exist other forms of public accountability.

This question has been most hotly debated in the case of the nationalized industries. When the majority of the nationalized industries were created after 1945, the model adopted was the arm's length approach whose architect was Herbert Morrison. The essence of this model is that ministers are responsible for policy but the boards of the industries are to be free from political interference on day-to-day matters of management. This blueprint was enshrined in the nationalization Acts by reserving to ministers powers to appoint and in certain situations dismiss the chairmen and members of the boards in charge of the running of the industries, the power to give general directions on matters affecting the national interest, the need for ministerial approval of certain programmes such as development or reorganization involving substantial capital expenditure, and the ability to request information at any time. Most importantly from a practical point of view, if an industry could not meet its financial obligation to break even, it was the government who had to provide the money. These provisions were intended to give ministers strategic powers of control but to leave the boards freedom to manage the industry within the framework set by the minister and in particular to fix the prices and wages within the industry. This model did not work according to plan. The nationalized industries were too important to be left alone, particularly in the area of prices and wages. If there was a major strike on the railways or in the mines, negotiations took place with union leaders who at one period were invited to No. 10 Downing Street to talks over beer and sandwiches. If there were elections in the offing, pressure was brought to prevent a price increase in a key industry. Mostly pressure was not exerted through a general direction having legal effect under the statute but by informal discussions between the chairman and the minister which were given the nickname of lunch-table directives. The minister would either have appointed the chairman or be in a position not to reappoint him, the term of office usually being for five years. Where the industry needed money, the minister would be in the most powerful position to twist the chairman's arm. Very few general directions were ever issued and it is doubtful whether they could have been legally given in many of the situations where pressure was brought to bear on specific issues. Labour governments used their powers to make particular industries perform social obligations which were financially uneconomic, e.g. build a power station which was not yet needed, to provide employment. Mr Heath's government used the nationalized industries as the spearhead of his incomes policy by making them keep prices down.

This political interference with the running of the industries blurred the responsibility for their management and efficiency and played havoc with their finances. It became accepted that an industry which was asked to perform unprofitable social obligations should be compensated by the government (Cmnd 3437, 1967), though the means and extent were often the subject of much controversy. In spite of this concession, it was generally recognized that the relationship between ministers and the nationalized industries was unsatisfactory. In 1976 an independent inquiry recommended a new approach (National Economic Development Office). Instead of the arm's length approach which it thought had broken down and which it rejected as inappropriate for industries so vital to the economy of the country, it recommended a new structure based on co-operation between ministers and industries in a new body (the Policy Council) to be inserted between the minister and the boards where mutually agreed policies would be hammered out. Concertation rather than separation between minister and industry was to be the key. The Labour government, significantly, rejected these recommendations as imposing an unnecessary additional layer between the minister and the board (Cmnd 7131, 1978). It also disputed that there could be a clear-cut distinction between strategic decisions to be taken by the Policy Council and managerial decisions to be taken by the board of the industry, but it eagerly embraced the committee's recommendation to give ministers a last-resort power to give specific and not just general directions, which it promised to use sparingly. This promise never had to be implemented because Mrs Thatcher's government which followed had a very different philosophy towards the nationalized industries.

In theory the Conservative government espoused a hands-off approach. The nationalized industries were to be treated like private industry and the aim was that they should all as soon as possible pay their way and not rely on government subsidies. This did not prevent governmental interference during the miners' strike of 1984–5 in spite of the government's declared policy of neutrality. The overriding constraint imposed by the government was the financial limit within which each industry had to work. These limits determined how much an industry could borrow, or, if it was profitable like the gas and electricity industries or the Post Office, how much money it had to pay back to the government. These limits were fixed with reference to the government's monetary policy and they in turn determined the prices which the industry had to charge. Thus the government's economic policy determined the prices which the consumer had to pay rather than the financial state of the industry. Non-interference by the government was therefore practised more in theory than reality.

The Conservative government's main solution to the problems arising from the relationship between the government and the nationalized industries is de-nationalization. The slogan is that the proper business of government is not the government of business. However, privatization has not eliminated the problem of governmental interference. The government still retains a stake in some industries, e.g. the 40% stake in the private electricity generating companies. Even where all the shares have been sold, the government may retain a special share to use in case of a foreign takeover or other emergency. The government has declared that it will treat these companies in the same way as a private sector company and will not use any shareholding it retains to interfere in the commercial decisions of the company except in the circumstances envisaged for the use of the special share. It does, however, retain the power to use its shareholding where this exists and a subsequent government would *a fortiori* not be bound by this declaration. The revelation of the pressures brought to bear on British Aerospace, in which the government only retained a special share, to withdraw from the European consortium which made a bid to take over Westland Helicopters, and the arm-twisting to which the fully private firm of Westland itself (as supplier of helicopters to the armed services) was subjected by both camps in the government make a mockery of the policy of non-interference with industry which the government professes. On the other hand in debates over the pit closures the government argued that it could not legally bring pressure on the electricity generating companies in which it held 40% of the shares to make them buy more coal so as to reprieve more pits (HL Deb., vol. 539, col. 675, 20 October 1992).

The pit closure issue illustrates that the government cannot opt-out of policy decisions of this magnitude. Though it was British Coal's responsibility to close down pits, the government had to face the political fall-out and to pick up the bill for redundancies and the resulting devastation in the mining communities. The pit closure issue also shows that privatization does not absolve the government from responsibility. It was the way in which the electricity industry was privatized that led to the 'dash for gas', i.e. the building of gas-fired power stations with the Secretary of State's consent which reduced the demand for coal. Again the levy on electricity produced from coal to subsidize nuclear power was imposed by the government. The government cannot interfere directly with the price of electricity which is fixed by a price formula contained in the licence granted by the Secretary of State and reviewed by a regulator who is appointed by the Secretary of State. A regulator has been appointed to monitor each of the privatized utilities and these regulators raise in a new form the same conflict between independence and accountability which bedevilled the nationalized industries. The electricity regulator was much criticised during the inquiry on pit closures by the Trade and Industry Committee which called for more control over regulators' discretionary powers by the government and Parliament (HC 237, 1992–3, para 293). One commentator on these new quangos asked: 'Is this going to be a way of privatizing what are on occasion political judgements?' (Walker, 1990, p. 157).

The area where this battle will be fought next is over the independence of the Bank of England *vis-à-vis* the government in respect of monetary policy. Mr Lamont in his resignation statement as Chancellor of the Exchequer cited his failure to persuade the Prime Minister to give the Bank independence as one of the crucial differences between them (HC Deb., vol. 226, col. 281, 9 June 1993). The Prime Minister said that he saw the case for an independent central bank and would support it if the benefits could be obtained without the loss of parliamentary accountability (ibid., col. 295). With this aim in view the Treasury and Civil Service Committee recommended a semi-independent Bank which would be responsible for achieving price stability within publicly-stated targets set by the government (HC 98, 1993–4). Independent national central banks are the precondition for the setting up of the independent European Central Bank which, like the national central banks, would not take instructions from anyone whether EC institutions or governments. This European system of central banks constitutes the third stage of Economic and Monetary Union (EMU), one of the crucial issues on which the UK negotiated an opt-out from the Maastricht Treaty. A special Act of Parliament will be necessary if Britain wants to move to this third stage of EMU (European Communities (Amendment) Act 1993, section 2).

The latest quango count revealed that, though the number of quangos has been reduced by about one-third since 1979, their expenditure has risen in real terms by about one-fifth (Public Bodies, 1993; Cabinet Office, 1994). There has also been the creation of new bodies in the areas of health and local government because of opting-out provisions for hospitals and schools and the provision of social housing. The most worrying aspect of this development is the scale of public money which such bodies can dispense (one-fifth of all public spending) and the scope for political patronage in respect of appointments to these bodies which has been amply exercised (HL Deb., vol. 551, col. 610, seq., 19 January 1994). Politically appointed quangos represent the worst of both worlds; they do not take decisions out of politics but they are not democratically accountable. In other words they exercise political power without political responsibility.

Local authorities

The relationship between the central government and local authorities is again a different one. Local authorities are the only public bodies apart from the House of Commons which are directly elected. Local councillors, therefore, represent and are accountable to their local electorate which gives them a legitimacy quite different from that of an appointed body and which can lead to direct conflict with central government, particularly one of a different political persuasion. However, in our constitution, whose linchpin is the sovereignty of Parliament, the central government with a majority in the House of Commons has the last word through being able to pass legislation. The increase in recent years of legislation to regulate the relationship between central and local government is indicative of its breakdown, as traditionally this has been based on consensus, consultation and co-operation rather than law.

Local authorities derive all their powers from Acts of Parliament in which the government of the day lays down its policy in respect of a particular subject-matter whether it be housing, education or town and country planning and delimits the functions which local authorities perform in that field. Local authorities in this country have no general powers to carry on activities outside their statutory powers, though they are entitled to spend a very small amount of their income for the benefit of the area or its inhabitants. Central government not only lays down the framework of powers and duties to be performed by local authorities but may impose detailed controls over their exercise. Local authority plans laying down their policy on a particular subject-matter may be made subject to ministerial guidance, e.g. development plans under the Town and Country Planning Acts. Again these Acts provide a right of appeal to the minister against a refusal of planning permission by a local authority. Similar ministerial powers exist in many other areas of local government. Bye-laws made by local authorities also need ministerial confirmation, and certain appointments need ministerial approval. In respect of some functions, e.g. police and social services, ministers have powers of inspection, and legislation often confers on ministers reserve powers to act where the local authority has failed to perform one of its functions. Ministers may also in some cases have power to give directions to local authorities or provide guidance for the exercise of a function, e.g. the provision of social services. An increasing number of Acts make provision for such guidance to be issued, which was formerly and is still in many cases provided without specific authority, usually in the form of a circular. As we have seen, such circulars have often been used as a means of persuading local authorities to adopt certain policies in preference to enacting legislation making such policies obligatory. The increasing use of legislation to impose central government's policies on local authorities indicates the breakdown of consensus, and nowhere is this more marked than in the case of local government finance whose control enables central government to wield most power over local authorities and which has given rise to the greatest conflict.

Local authorities derive their finance from locally raised revenue, central government grants, charges and fees, and in the case of capital expenditure mainly from loans and capital receipts. The main conflict between central and local government in recent years has arisen over the attempt, particularly by Mrs Thatcher's government, to control local government expenditure in furtherance of the government's economic policies. The previous Labour government had tried to curb local authorities' current expenditure by imposing strict limits to prevent the central government grant increasing in line with local expenditure and by reducing the total grant available to all authorities if they collectively overshot the totals of expenditure indicated by central government. The Conservative government changed the law in the Local Government, Planning and Land Act 1980 so as to enable the grant allocated to individual authorities to be tailored to reflect the extent to which they complied with the figure which the central government department determined to be the correct expenditure for each authority, so that increases in expenditure above a certain level attracted less grant. Even though this figure was not legally binding, it represented an inroad on the autonomy of local authorities to determine their own expenditure. Control was further tightened in 1982. When these measures did not have the desired effect because local authorities could make good the shortfall of income from government grant by levying higher rates to finance their expenditure, the government in the Rates Act 1984 took powers to impose rate-capping on local authorities which allowed the minister to fix the maximum rates of those authorities who spent above another set of limits laid down by the minister. Thus power of a local authority to fix its own rates was for the first time interfered with by central government. The rates as such came under attack next. Mrs Thatcher had given a pledge to abolish the rates when she was Leader of the Opposition and when the revaluation of properties on which rates were levied caused an outcry in Scotland, the pledge was honoured and Scotland became the guinea pig for the hated community charge which contributed so much to Mrs Thatcher's downfall. Its rationale and hence its nickname poll tax was that everyone, however poor, should pay something towards local government expenditure, unlike rates, which were levied only on occupiers of property. The rhetoric for the poll tax stressed accountability and fairness, namely that all those who could vote for local expenditure should have to pay towards it and that a person living alone should not have to pay the same as the household of several adults living next door. The reality was the gross unfairness of a flat-rate charge which was unrelated to income and the 20% charge on students and those on income support which led to poll tax riots and enormous enforcement problems with millions of summonses to non-payers, many of whom disenfranchised themselves by removing themselves from the electoral register to avoid detection, with profound consequences for democracy.

The poll tax was introduced in April 1990; Mrs Thatcher was deposed in November 1990 and in the 1991 Budget VAT was increased to 17½% to pay for a poll tax rebate of £140 per head. The Bill providing for the new council tax to replace the poll tax was rushed through the House of Commons after its introduction in November 1991. It was most unusually guillotined immediately after its second reading and the Standing Committee which considered the Bill in detail sat late into the night. The tax tried to avoid the pitfalls of the poll tax without jettisoning it completely. It, therefore, returned to a property-based tax but retained a personal element in the form of a discount for single person households. The tax is levied on domestic properties which are divided into 8 bands according to their capital value so that those in the highest band pay three times as much tax as those in the lowest band. This removed the unfairness of the flat-rate poll tax to some extent, though the differential between the top and the bottom band was skewed in favour of the better off. The tax was based on a two person household thus deliberately not charging large households more tax unlike the poll tax. There was also abandonment of the principle that all voters must pay something by abolishing the 20% levy on students and those on income support. The main survivor from the poll tax principle was the discount for single person households. To prevent verification of this discount, which has to be claimed, it was feared voters would remove themselves from the electoral register but the incentive to do this is far less than under the poll tax and the problems of collecting a tax from householders should be far fewer than under the poll tax.

There has quite deliberately been no change under the council tax to the amount of local government expenditure to be funded from the tax in relation to other sources of revenue, such as the rate levied on business property which is fixed by the government and the grant paid by central government. This is assessed on the basis of what the government thinks each local authority should spend, the issue which began the assault on local government expenditure in 1980. Since the council tax now funds only about one-fifth of local government expenditure it will have to rise very steeply for every pound of expenditure over the amount calculated as necessary by the government. Such rises will be capped by the government, a power the government did not abolish together with the rates. Local authorities inevitably have to reduce their expenditure in line with government policy which was the original objective. The result is another step towards more centralized government.

There has been an even more fundamental assault on local government than the financial stranglehold by central government. The government is intent on transforming local authorities from being providers of services to enabling others to provide them and sees the role of local authorities as setting standards and monitoring performance (Consultation Paper:

The Structure of Local Government in England, 1991). This revolution has been accomplished through privatization in various forms of local authority services. The selling of council houses, the opting-out of schools which become grant-maintained and the contracting out of services through competitive tendering are all aspects of this development. Even the police are not immune from proposals for putting out to private tender many of their functions (*Guardian*, 11 July 1994). This transformation of the functions of local government has been used to support the case for the reorganization of the structure of local government less than twenty years after the last major upheaval of local authorities in 1974. Because of the changing role of local authorities the government argued that there is now no ideal size which an authority must have to deliver services (Consultation Paper, 1991 (supra) para. 21). There was also no need for a uniform structure, though the government clearly favours single tier, i.e. unitary authorities which is the existing structure in London and the metropolitan areas outside London after the abolition of the Greater London Council and the metropolitan county councils in 1985 (ibid., para. 25 seq.). A Local Government Commission for England has been set up to review the structure of local authorities in England area by area in accordance with guidance from the Secretary of State for the Environment. The creation of new unitary authorities in most areas will inevitably lead, as it did in London and the metropolitan areas, to the creation of joint authorities, new quangos and more central government control because the authorities will be too small to carry out particular functions. It is already clear that both fire brigades and police forces will be further amalgamated and the Home Secretary will have power to prescribe national objectives for the police service but his power to appoint the chairmen of local police authorities had to be dropped from the Police and Magistrates' Court Bill 1994 as a result of pressure from the House of Lords (HL Deb., vol. 552, col. 941 seq., 1 March 1994). The missing link in the restructuring of local government in England is a tier of elected regional government which would have a strategic and coordinating role for the new local authorities and to whom power could be devolved from central government.

The pressure for devolution of power from central government has been strongest in Scotland and Wales to which the government has responded in the case of Scotland with provisions for more power for the Scottish Office and the expansion of the functions of the House of Commons Scottish Grand Committee on which all Scottish MPs sit (Cm 2225, 1993). It has firmly resisted the creation of elected national assemblies for either Scotland or Wales. Its proposals for the reorganization of local government in these countries in favour of unitary authorities have now been implemented by the Local Government (Scotland) and the Local Government (Wales) Acts 1994, but as in England there will be no intermediate tier of government between these authorities and the central government. So far as the UK is concerned, subsidiarity, i.e. that decisions should be taken as locally as possible, one of the key principles of the Maastricht Treaty, is only applied to the British government but not to the countries and regions of the UK. Subsidiarity does not begin at home.

4

CONTROL MECHANISMS
AND PUBLIC ACCOUNTABILITY

There are a number of mechanisms whereby those who exercise the functions discussed in the previous chapter can be supervised, monitored and held to account. The courts, though numerically they deal with only a small number of cases, are perhaps constitutionally the most significant because the subjection of public authorities to the ordinary courts is the cornerstone of the rule of law as formulated by Dicey in his *Law of the Constitution* (1885, Chapter IV).

COURTS

The courts cannot act as courts of appeal from any of the bodies examined in the previous chapter unless there are express statutory provisions to this effect. They do, however, possess the power to review the decisions of such bodies unless there are express statutory provisions excluding judicial control. Judicial review is more limited than appeal as it is not concerned with the merits of the decision but with its propriety, though in practice the distinction may be a fine one.

Judicial review

The proper remedy for reviewing the actions of public authorities is an application for judicial review, but where the applicant's private rights are infringed by a public body the private law remedies of declaration and injunction still apply

(*O'Reilly v. Mackman*, 1983). There are important procedural differences between an application for judicial review and the other remedies, which provide safeguards for the public authority whose decision is being challenged. Leave has to be obtained from a judge for the application to proceed. There are strict time-limits within which proceedings must be started and cases are heard by a judge drawn from specialists in administrative law. Evidence is presented in the form of written affidavits rather than orally through witnesses, a procedure which is not suitable for resolving disputed questions of fact, which will not normally be at issue in such proceedings. The applicant must have a sufficient interest in bringing the proceedings which means that he must be more than a mere busybody, but whether a taxpayer has such an interest has given rise to much controversy (*Inland Revenue Commissioners v. National Federation of Self-Employed*, 1982, and *R. v. Her Majesty's Treasury ex parte Smedley*, 1985), as has the position of pressure groups (*R. v Secretary of State for Social Services ex parte Child Poverty Action Group*, 1990 and *R. v. Secretary of State for the Environment ex parte Rose Theatre Trust Co.*, 1990). All these procedural issues are now being examined by the Law Commission (Law Commission Paper, 1993 – Administrative Law: Judicial Review and Statutory Appeals).

The grounds on which judicial review may be allowed have been categorized by Lord Diplock in his judgement in *Council of Civil Service Unions v. Minister for the Civil Service* (1984: *GCHQ* case) where judicial review was requested of the Prime Minister's instruction prohibiting staff employed in the Government Communications Headquarters to be members of a trade union. He classified the grounds for judicial review under three headings, namely, illegality, irrationality and procedural impropriety. The case decides that the same grounds of review are available whether the powers are derived from statute or from the residual common law powers of the Crown (the prerogative), as in the case itself, though they may not be applicable to such prerogative powers as the dissolution of Parliament or the granting of honours. However, in *R. v. Secretary of State for the Home*

Department ex parte Bentley (1994), it was held that even the royal prerogative of mercy, i.e. to grant a pardon to someone who has been convicted, is reviewable by the courts.

ILLEGALITY

Under the heading of illegality Lord Diplock said, 'the decision-maker must understand correctly the law that regulates his decision-making power and must give effect to it' (*GCHQ*, p. 1196). The difficulty is to distinguish a mistake of law that regulates the decision-making power (error going to jurisdiction) from a mistake of law which the decision-maker has the authority to determine (error of law). The distinction between the law which delimits the jurisdiction of the decision-maker and that which is within his jurisdiction was for practical purposes eliminated in the *Anisminic* case (1969) when a decision of the Foreign Compensation Commission, a body set up to distribute compensation for property expropriated abroad, was declared invalid for misconstruction of provisions it was supposed to interpret, although the decisions were expressly declared in the statute as not being open to challenge in any court. By holding that the decision of the Commission was void, the House of Lords set aside the exclusion clause. As a result of the decision any error of law of a decision-making body is open to judicial review. Taken to its logical conclusion this would enable the courts on an application for judicial review to sit in judgement on the interpretation of all the statutory provisions and those contained in delegated legislation which has been entrusted to the various types of decision-making bodies. In practice the courts have not used their powers to the full extent. They may categorize the error as one of fact rather than law where the words to be interpreted are ordinary, non-technical English words, and may leave their interpretation to be determined by the inferior body unless the interpretation is so unreasonable that no reasonable body could reach it, when it would fall within Lord Diplock's second ground of irrationality. The courts will also adopt this approach where they feel the question of interpretation is more suitable for an expert body, which has been set up by Parliament for this purpose, than for the courts. It is, however, very difficult to predict when the courts will adopt the hands-off approach and when they will reinterpret the relevant provisions themselves. This is where extra-legal considerations come into play and the attitude of the judiciary towards questions of social policy may be the hidden premise on which the decision is based.

The attitude of the courts towards issues of policy may be quite explicit when they lay down criteria which the decision-maker must take into account but which are not mentioned in the statutory provisions and may directly contradict statutory provisions which give wide discretionary powers to a body to act as it thinks fit. These limitations which the courts superimpose on statutory provisions may be explicitly designed to protect individual rights, e.g. not to be deprived of access to the courts. Thus the courts will, as we saw in the *Anisminic* case, construe any statutory provision to this effect as narrowly as possible, though even here the attitude is not consistent and they have held to be judge-proof clauses which exclude judicial control after six weeks, e.g. in the case of compulsory purchase orders, where a reopening of the decision would cause administrative chaos (*R. v. Secretary of State for the Environment ex parte Ostler*, 1977). The courts will also narrowly construe a power to levy a charge from the citizen so that express provision is necessary and even wide discretionary powers will not be sufficient authorization. Thus a wide power to control food supplies under regulations made to secure the public safety and the defence of the realm did not include a power to charge for the issue of a licence to purchase milk (*AG v. Wiltshire United Dairies*, 1921), and a power to revoke a television licence by a notice in writing did not give the Home Secretary power to revoke a licence which had been renewed before the expiry of the old one so as to avoid paying the increased fee (*Congreve v. Home Office*, 1976).

Similarly the courts have construed legislation and wide discretionary powers exercised under it so as not to take away property rights. The attitude of the judiciary towards great issues of social policy such as slum clearance, council housing and town and country planning can be plotted according to how they have interpreted the legislation *vis-à-vis* the property owner. This has fluctuated from periods of intense hostility to the Housing Acts in the 1930s to a period of acquiescence in town and country planning legislation after 1945 until a reaction set in in the late 1950s when the courts reasserted private property rights in a spate of decisions which emasculated the Town and Country Planning Acts. Parliament engaged in a running battle with the courts at these times, amending the statutes so as to prevent the courts from misinterpreting the legislation, but the courts have the last word on interpretation. The courts can thus limit the ambit of social legislation by superimposing their policy conceptions based on individual rights when interpreting a statute.

Perhaps the most striking illustration of the courts reading limitations into statutory provisions so as to narrow the discretionary powers conferred under them is the duty the courts impose on local authorities to hold the balance between their local taxpayers and other sections of the community. This was one of the grounds on which the GLC's Fares Fair policy, which cut London Transport's fares, was declared unlawful by the courts in *Bromley London Borough Council v. GLC* (1982). Similarly in 1925 in *Roberts v. Hopwood* it was held on the same principle unlawful for a local authority to exercise its powers to pay such wages as it thought fit by paying all its workers male and female a minimum of £4 a week, which was excessive by commercial standards at that time. In contrast the courts held in 1983 in *Pickwell v. Camden London Borough Council* that Camden Borough Council had not acted unlawfully when it settled a strike of manual workers by agreeing a figure above that at which a national settlement was later negotiated. The court said that it was not the basic legal principle which had changed but our attitudes. The real issue is whether the attitude of the courts should prevail over that of the elected local authority in exercising a discretionary power. In the *Camden* case, unlike the *GLC* case and *Roberts v. Hopwood*, the court bent over backwards not to interfere with the judgement of the elected body.

To what extent this power of the courts to read limitations into statutory provisions will be affected by the seminal decision of *Pepper v. Hart* (1992) remains to be seen. In this case the House of Lords reversed the rule that the courts cannot look at the record of Parliamentary proceedings in Hansard as an aid to statutory interpretation. It held (with the Lord Chancellor dissenting) that reference to Parliamentary material should be permitted where the statute is ambiguous or obscure or the literal meaning would lead to an absurdity and the statement made in Parliament by the minister or the promoter of a Bill makes it clear what the words were intended to mean. In the case itself all these criteria were satisfied as the very point in issue was dealt with by a minister in Standing Committee. This is unlikely to be the case where the courts read limitations into broad statutory provisions.

IRRATIONALITY

Lord Diplock's second ground of judicial review in the *GCHQ* case (1984) is irrationality, which he defines as unreasonableness in accordance with the principles of the *Wednesbury* case (1948), i.e. 'a decision which is so outrageous in its defiance of logic or of accepted moral standards that no sensible person who had applied his mind to the question to be decided could have arrived at it' (*GCHQ*, p. 1196). This principle was construed very narrowly in the *Camden* case so as not to interfere with the judgement of the local authority. However, in the *Secretary of State for Education v. Tameside Borough Council* (1977) the courts had the unenviable task of having to judge the unreasonableness of the decisions of two elected authorities, the minister and the local authority who were in conflict. The Secretary of State for Education had power to give a direction to a local authority which he was satisfied was acting unreasonably. He gave such a direction to the local authority who, after a local election which the Conservatives won, overturned the decision of their Labour predecessors to adopt comprehensive education and abolish grammar schools. The minister thought there was insufficient time to implement the new selection process before the beginning of the school year. The court applied the very narrow test of unreasonableness to the local authority's actions which had just been approved by the electorate. On the other hand, they held that the minister had no grounds for finding that the local authority had acted unreasonably and that no reasonable minister could so find. This seems to be applying differing tests of unreasonableness to the minister and the local authority. In contrast to this case the Secretary of State for the Environment was held to be acting reasonably when he used his default powers against Norwich City Council (*R. v. Secretary of State for the Environment ex parte Norwich City Council*, 1982) because of their policy of passive resistance to the sale of council houses. As these cases illustrate, the courts have in recent years been used increasingly as the forum where the conflict between local and central government is being fought out. This has escalated in the area of local government finance where in case upon case the courts have been asked to interpret the complicated provisions of the successive statutes which tighten the financial noose round local authorities. In one of the most important of these cases which challenged the legality of the whole system of targets under the Local Government Finance Act 1982 (*R. v. Secretary of State for the Environment ex parte Nottinghamshire County Council*, 1986) the House of Lords, reversing the Court of Appeal, upheld the decision of the minister. Lord Scarman, with whom the rest of the court agreed, held that in this case, where the minister's decision had to be approved by the House of Commons, 'it is not for the judges to say that the action has such unreasonable consequences that the guidance upon which the action is based and of which the House of Commons had notice was perverse and must be set aside. For that is a question of policy for the minister and the Commons, unless there has been bad faith or misconduct by the minister' (pp. 7–8). Even more pointedly, Lord Templeman said, 'Judicial review is not just a move in an interminable chess tournament. Although I do not blame Nottingham or Bradford for instituting these proceedings, I hope that in future local authorities will bite on the bullet and not seek to persuade the courts to absolve them from compliance with the Secretary of State's guidance. If for any particular city or for any group of cities guidance is set too low, having regard to their peculiar needs, then persuasion should be offered not to the judges, who are not qualified to listen, but to the department, the minister, all members of parliament and ultimately to the electorate' (p. 23). This impeccable constitutional advice has, however, fallen on deaf ears and the challenge to the decision to impose a cap on some local authorities to reduce the level of their poll tax predictably failed (*R. v. Secretary of State for the Environment ex parte Hammersmith and Fulham London Borough Council*, 1990). When ministers refuse to give way, Parliament is whipped and the General Election is years ahead, the courts become the political arena because the political remedies do not work. This makes it very difficult for the judges to remain above the political battle, for even judicial abstention, as in the *Nottingham* case, can be seen as taking sides. In our constitution based on the sovereignty of Parliament it is a sign of breakdown of the political system when the courts are used as a political battle-ground.

PROCEDURAL IMPROPRIETY

Lord Diplock's third ground of judicial review is concerned with challenge to the procedure by which the decision is reached rather than with its substance. In practice this may often be the only line of attack open to an applicant who wants a decision to which he objects set aside, because he cannot challenge the decision on its merits by judicial review. The quashing of the decision may be a pyrrhic victory as a new decision may be taken after following the correct procedure but in many cases the victory will in practice be final.

The procedural impropriety may be the result of not following procedural rules laid down by statute or delegated legislation, though the courts will not construe every minor failure to observe such provisions as grounds for striking down such a decision.

Though most tribunals and public inquiries are regulated by procedural rules, many decisions made by ministers, local authorities and other public bodies are not regulated by statutory procedures. It is in this area that the courts have been most creative in fashioning principles to which those who make decisions affecting individuals must conform. The most famous principles are the rules of natural justice which have been applied to a constantly expanding area of decision-making. Though originally the courts distinguished these rules from the more flexible concept of procedural fairness, they are now often treated as synonymous, their application varying according to the subject-matter of the decision. Out of these rules the courts have now developed a new concept of procedural propriety where a legitimate expectation of the applicant is withdrawn.

There are two rules of natural justice which the courts have formulated, namely that no one may be a judge in his own cause and that a person affected by a decision must be given an opportunity to state his case and one person must not be heard behind the back of the other. These basic moral principles, allegedly derived from the Old Testament, have given rise to a myriad of cases to determine their application in a vast variety of situations.

The first rule of natural justice is a rule against bias in the decision-maker, who should have no personal or pecuniary interest in the decision. This rule, which, like its twin, is modelled on the judicial process, caused particular difficulty in relation to decisions of ministers who had to hold a public inquiry into objections against a decision made by themselves, e.g. to build a road or designate a new town, and ultimately had to decide whether to confirm their own decision after having heard the objectors. Bias in favour of their own decision was built into the decision-making process and the courts held in the famous case concerning Stevenage New Town, *Franklin v. Minister of Town and Country Planning* (1948), that so long as the minister gave genuine consideration to the objections raised at the inquiry he could be as biased in favour of building a new town at Stevenage as he liked. A minister making a policy decision could not be forced into the straitjacket of a judge.

Similar problems were encountered in applying the second rule of natural justice to ministerial decisions reached after public inquiries. In another landmark decision, *Local Government Board v. Arlidge* (1915), it was held that the inspector's report to the minister after the inquiry did not have to be disclosed. This decision has now been reversed by the statutory rules regulating the procedure of inquiries which are made under the Tribunals and Inquiries Act 1992. These regulations are a statutory embodiment of the rules of natural justice applicable to public inquiries but problems of their interpretation still have to be decided by the courts and, where an inquiry is not regulated by rules, they are still called upon to adapt the rules of natural justice to a policy decision reached by a judicialized procedure. Thus in *Bushell v. Secretary of State for the Environment* (1980) the House of Lords had to decide whether the methodology for making traffic predictions for a new road was a question of fact and therefore open to cross-examination or a matter of policy on which cross-examination was rightly disallowed. In deciding the latter they were very much influenced by the view that a motorway inquiry is part of the policy-making process rather than a trial.

The cases relating to public inquiries were regarded as in a special category by Lord Reid in *Ridge v. Baldwin* (1964), the case which was the springboard from which the expansion of natural justice took off. The courts had before that case limited the application of the rules of natural justice to deprivation of rights rather than privileges and had not applied them to the exercise of wide discretionary powers or the exercise of disciplinary functions. In *Ridge v. Baldwin* the House of Lords declared void the dismissal of the Chief Constable of Brighton because he had not been offered an opportunity to present his case, his dismissal being based on what he himself and the judge had said at his trial on a charge of corruption of which he was acquitted. The court brushed aside the decisions which had narrowed the application of natural justice and, basing itself on earlier decisions, held that where there must be something against a man before he could be dismissed from an office, as in this case, the rules of natural justice had to be observed.

The block having been removed, the way was open to apply the rules of natural justice to an ever expanding category of cases. One of these has been university students who have been held entitled to the benefit of the rules of natural justice before having their course terminated (*R. v. Aston University ex parte Roffey*, 1969) or being suspended from the university (*Glynn v. Keele*

University, 1971), although in both cases the courts refused a remedy in the exercise of their discretion because of the facts of the cases. More recently the courts have broken open the prison gates and applied the rules of natural justice in favour of prisoners in the case of the hearing of charges against discipline (*R. v. Visitors of Hull Prison ex parte St Germain*, 1979 and *Leech v. Deputy Governor of Parkhurst Prison*, 1988) and even in respect of the first period (the penal element) of a life sentence for murder (*R. v. Secretary of State for the Home Department ex parte Doody*, 1993). Where issues of national security are involved, the courts have refused to apply the rules of natural justice, e.g. in the case of a deportation order based on this ground (*R. v. Home Secretary ex parte Hosenball*, 1977 and *R. v. Secretary of State for the Home Department ex parte Cheblak*, 1991).

The courts have also varied the content of the rules in accordance with the circumstances of the case. They can include the duty to give reasons, the right to legal representation and the right to cross-examine witnesses at an oral hearing or merely an opportunity to make representations without knowing all the evidence against one or the source of the information. This attenuated form of natural justice is sometimes referred to as a duty to act fairly but these terms are also treated as synonymous. Recently the duty to act fairly has been applied to cases where a person has a 'legitimate expectation'. This vague concept has been applied to a number of situations such as the revocation of a permit before it has expired, the remission of a sentence and, as we saw, the statement in a Home Office circular of the circumstances when an adopted child would be allowed into this country. The most famous application of the concept was in the *GCHQ* case when the House of Lords held that the trade unions at GCHQ had a legitimate expectation based on past practice to be consulted about the ban on employees from being members of a trade union. This right to be consulted was, however, in the circumstances of the case negated in the interests of national security. But it was successfully asserted in one of the many cases concerning local government finance, enabling a number of London borough councils to have the decision reducing their grant declared invalid because the minister had refused to hear further representations (*R. v. Secretary of State for the Environment ex parte Brent LBC*, 1982). The victory was pyrrhic for one authority because the minister, having listened to further representations, still withheld the grant (*R. v. Secretary of State for the Environment ex parte Hackney LBC*, 1983). The concept of legitimate expectation has extended the principle of fairness to a category of cases where natural justice had not previously been applied and has thus advanced the cause of open government, though at the expense of slowing down the process of policy-making. This was dramatically illustrated by the judicial review proceedings to halt the pit closures announced by the President of the Board of Trade in October 1992. The court held that the trade unions and their members had a legitimate expectation that the colliery review procedure, which had been agreed after the miners' strike in 1985, would be used and the decision was, therefore, unlawful (*R. v. President of the Board of Trade ex parte NUM etc. Guardian*, 22 December 1992). This was, however, again a pyrrhic victory as in May 1993 the court reversed its earlier decision because no agreement could be reached between British Coal and the NUM on an independent review procedure and British Coal had allowed independent scrutiny of its proposals (*The Times* Law Reports, 28 May 1993). A legitimate expectation to be consulted may also be inapplicable when immediate decisions have to be made. The Law Society's challenge of the regulations cutting the number of people eligible for legal aid failed on this ground (*Guardian*, 22 June 1993).

A legitimate expectation giving a right to natural justice may also arise from an express promise, but the promise is not binding as such. The courts have evolved a principle of public law which says that a public authority cannot fetter the exercise of its discretionary powers by a promise to act in a particular way even if this has been relied upon to his detriment by the person to whom the promise is made. A public authority must be able to change its policy in the public interest even at the expense of a private individual. Thus it was held in *Laker Airways Ltd v.*

Department of Trade (1977) that the government was entitled to change its policy about the licence granted to Mr Laker to run Skytrain to the USA, even though he had suffered loss by relying on previous representations, because a government must be allowed to change its policy (Lord Denning dissented on this point). However, the government's policy decision was declared invalid on other grounds.

Similarly, a government may not fetter its own discretion by laying down rules for its exercise unless it is prepared to hear representations from anyone that the rule should be changed or not apply to him. This ensures that discretion is exercised on the facts of each case and was another ground on which the London borough councils won their case against the reduction of their grant, for the minister had refused to listen to any further representations. This rule is the converse of the legitimate expectation rule which prevents the public authority from changing its mind without first giving those affected an opportunity to make representations. One rule is in favour of flexibility, the other is in favour of the status quo.

Thus the courts have fashioned a battery of principles through which they can impose their values on public authorities. The government can by legislation reverse any decision of the courts, which is done almost as a matter of routine now, but it cannot easily eradicate the principles on which judicial control is based. Perhaps this should be regarded as the true meaning of the rule of law. However, the decision in *Pepper v. Hart* (supra) could have a profound effect on the relationship between the courts and the Executive. If a ministerial statement can in certain cases predetermine the interpretation of a statute, it will be an important breach in the separation of powers between the courts and the Executive and will downgrade the function of the judiciary. Paradoxically the case has already prompted a broadside from the Speaker of the House of Commons (HC Deb., vol. 229, col. 353, 21 July 1993) warning the courts to fully respect the Bill of Rights 1689, which prohibited the courts from questioning proceedings in Parliament, when hearing the legal challenge by Lord Rees-Mogg to prevent the government ratifying the Maastricht Treaty (supra p. 48). The court rejected any suggestion that the action trespassed on proceedings in Parliament.

PARLIAMENTARY COMMISSIONER FOR ADMINISTRATION

The Parliamentary Commissioner for Administration (PCA) or Ombudsman, as he is popularly called, was set up under the Parliamentary Commissioner Act 1967 in response to pressure which began in 1954 with the Crichel Down affair, the classic illustration of maladministration by civil servants, for which the only remedy was to bring political and parliamentary pressure on the minister who eventually set up an inquiry to investigate the affair, which, as we saw, led to his resignation. Since this machinery cannot be set in motion for every mistake made in a government department, an aggrieved individual is left without a remedy apart from writing to his MP. The Franks Committee, which was set up in the wake of the Crichel Down affair, was only empowered to consider the workings of tribunals and inquiries and did not, therefore, include the ordinary administrative process of a government department. The catalyst which gave the impetus for the establishment of the PCA was a report commissioned in 1961 by JUSTICE, a private organization consisting of lawyers, which remodelled the Scandinavian institution of the Ombudsman by reference to the British Comptroller and Auditor General and recommended the creation of a Parliamentary Commissioner for Administration.

The hallmark of the PCA which distinguishes his office from that of the Ombudsman is its parliamentary nature. This is the rationale which underlies the whole institution and gives it its distinctive flavour. It is responsible for one of the main limitations peculiar to the British institution, namely that complaints must come through an MP rather than directly from the aggrieved citizen. This has not prevented individuals from approaching the PCA directly and he receives about the same number of complaints by this route as through MPs (i.e. over nine hundred annually). The PCA can now offer to send such cases to the MP, who can then ask him to investigate, but this procedure has only been used in a small proportion of cases because most of these complaints fall outside the PCA's jurisdiction (HC 615, 1977–8: Report of Select Committee on the PCA).

The narrowness of the PCA's jurisdiction is probably the greatest limitation on the office. The complaint must be one of maladministration resulting in injustice in connection with action taken by a government department or other body to which the Act applies, provided it is not in one of the excepted categories listed in the Act. Large areas of administration are thus excluded from the PCA's remit, though the gaps may be filled by other institutions. Thus the exclusion of local authorities is now made good by the establishment of Local Commissioners for Administration in 1974 who perform similar functions *vis-à-vis* local authorities. Complaints against the police are now supervised by the Police Complaints Authority set up under the Police and Criminal Evidence Act 1984. The PCA himself has been appointed as Health Service Commissioner, who since 1973 performs similar functions to the PCA in relation to the National Health Service. Governments have rejected the extension of the PCA's ambit to the nationalized industries on the grounds that they are commercial bodies and have their own complaints machinery. The government in 1985 accepted recommendations to include about fifty quangos within the PCA's jurisdiction including such bodies as the British Council, the Commission for Racial Equality and Equal Opportunities Commission and the London Docklands Development Corporation, thus increasing the public accountability of these bodies (Parliamentary and Health Service Commissioners Act 1987). Many more bodies have been added since that date. After a long battle the administrative actions of those court and tribunal staff appointed by the Lord Chancellor and the administrative staff of certain tribunals were also brought within the PCA's jurisdiction (Courts and Legal Services Act 1990 and Parliamentary Commissioner Act 1994). The executive agencies which now constitute such a large part of the civil service also fall within the remit of the PCA, as do those functions which have been contracted out to private contractors (Annual Report of the PCA for 1993, para. 8). The present PCA would like to see all public bodies which are funded by public money within his jurisdiction unless they are expressly excluded.

Some of the excluded categories of cases have also been the subject of controversy, in particular the exclusion of personnel matters in relation to the armed forces and civil servants. Governments have steadfastly refused to extend the PCA's jurisdiction to these cases on the grounds that other employees do not have access to the PCA for their grievances and that there are other mechanisms available for their redress. The other controversial exclusion is for contractual and other commercial transactions. This excludes the whole area of government contracting, even though this has been used for political purposes as happened when the government blacklisted and refused to give government contracts to those firms which broke its incomes policy from 1975 to 1978. It also bars him from investigating the giving of assistance to industry under wide discretionary powers but includes within his remit assistance which applicants expect to receive (Cmnd 7449, 1979). There was also controversy over whether Social Fund Officers who make decisions about lump sum payments from the Social Fund come within the PCA's jurisdiction but complaints about the operation of the Social Fund are being investigated.

The main limitation on the PCA's jurisdiction prevents him questioning the merits of a decision taken without maladministration (Parliamentary Commissioner Act 1967, section 12(3)). Maladministration is not defined in the Act but Mr Crossman when introducing the Bill said it included bias, neglect, inattention, delay, incompetence, ineptitude, perversity, turpitude, arbitrariness. The PCA has now rephrased this catalogue in the language of the 1990s (Annual Report for 1993, para. 7). More succinctly, the first PCA drew the distinction between the processes by which the decision was reached and the quality of the decision itself (HC 6, 1967–8). Nevertheless, the distinction is a fine one and it was further blurred by his following the recommendation of the select committee, to whom he reports, which wanted him to exercise jurisdiction over a perverse decision and where an administrative rule led to hardship (HC 350, 1967–8). Some of the PCA's most famous cases have been on the borderline between maladministration and the merits of a decision. Among his first cases were British prisoners of war who had been kept in German concentration camps and had been refused compensation provided by the German government and distributed by the Foreign Office. The view had been taken that they did not fall within the rules which had been drawn up by the Foreign Office for its distribution. The PCA criticized this decision (HC 54, 1967–8) and the complainants were granted compensation by George Brown, the Foreign Secretary at the time, but he rejected the PCA's criticisms and questioned whether the PCA's judgement was better than that of all the Foreign Secretaries who had dealt with the problem (HC Deb., vol. 758, col. 115, 5 February 1968). Similarly, in the case of Court Line, a company which was given financial assistance by Mr Benn, the PCA criticized the wording of the minister's statement to the House of Commons about the company as misleading (HC 498, 1974–5). Again this criticism was rejected by the minister because these were issues of policy on which the government had to make a judgement rather than the PCA (HC Deb., vol. 897, col. 582, 6 August 1975). The most recent *cause célèbre* where the same thing happened was the Barlow Clowes affair. Investors in the company, who lost their money when it went into liquidation, claimed that the Department of Trade and Industry were to blame for licensing the company, failing to revoke the licence and delaying an investigation into its affairs. The PCA found maladministration because of the lack of a sufficiently rigorous and enquiring approach by the Department (HC 76, 1989–90). The government rejected this finding and pointed out that the PCA should not criticize the merits of a decision. Nevertheless it agreed to pay £150 million compensation without admission of fault out of respect for the office of the PCA (HC 99, 1989–90). These cases show the danger of the PCA stepping outside his jurisdiction and becoming embroiled in highly controversial political issues. The risk is that he then becomes a political football who is used by the opposition to attack the government but whose reports are in consequence rejected by the government as not being within his terms of reference. Nevertheless, these cases are good for his public image.

On the other hand, they weaken his position which is based on acceptance of his reports, not on enforcement. The PCA has no powers except to make reports. The report on the individual case is sent to the MP who forwarded the complaint and to the Department and individual who were the subject of the complaint. An annual report and periodical reports with detailed cases are made to the House of Commons where they are referred to the Select Committee on the PCA. Special reports may be made on *causes célèbres* such as the case of the prisoners of war (*Sachsenhausen* case) and the *Court Line* and *Barlow Clowes* cases. The only back-up power the PCA has, if he thinks that an injustice has not been remedied following his report, is to make a special report to the House of Commons (1967 Act, section 10(3)). This has happened in only one case so far (HC 598, 1977–8) on which the PCA had to back-track later (HC 91, 1978–9). This does not mean, as we have seen in the *Court Line* case, that his recommendations are always accepted, though this does happen in the vast majority of cases. It does, however, illustrate that the PCA gets his way through persuasion and sometimes negotiation with the Department, which may change its mind during the course of the investigation.

The Select Committee on the PCA, which was set up by the House of Commons and survived the reorganization of select committees in 1979, plays an important part in bringing pressure to bear on government departments. It does not reinvestigate individual cases but considers the annual and special reports of the PCA by questioning the departments which are most frequently complained against, i.e. the Department of Social Security and the Inland Revenue. It monitors the extent to which complaints have been remedied and how far defects of administration highlighted in the reports have been put right. It is also concerned with reviewing the jurisdiction of the PCA and, as we have seen, has brought about important extensions of his terms of reference. It has recently conducted a wide-ranging inquiry into the work, powers and jurisdiction of the PCA (HC 33-I, 1993–4). It forms the most important pressure group for the PCA, though it has exceptionally, criticized the PCA himself for delay in handling a complaint, which, ironically, is one of the classic illustrations of maladministration (HC 312, 1985–6).

The average time taken for the investigation of complaints is over twelve months, a figure which conceals enormous variations between individual complaints. Delay is largely the result of the PCA's method of investigation which has been described as a Rolls-Royce method. Those complaints, which are settled as a result of an informal enquiry, are not counted as investigations. When the PCA decides to investigate, which he only does in about two hundred cases annually, as most cases referred to him fall outside his jurisdiction, his staff conduct a very thorough investigation through interviews and by examining departmental files. His powers of investigation are very wide. He has power to call for information from the minister downwards and he has access to all documents except those relating to the Cabinet (1967 Act, section 8). The thoroughness of his investigations accounts for the size of his staff (about one hundred) which is much greater than that of most other ombudsmen. Most of his staff are seconded from the civil service, and their working methods are again modelled on the Comptroller and Auditor General's office. Unlike other ombudsmen, the PCA has only two lawyers on his staff, although two PCAs have themselves been lawyers in contrast to the others who were civil servants.

The parliamentary connection of the PCA profoundly affects the publicity for his office and, therefore, his public image. His individual reports are not given to the press but to the MPs who may decide to inform the press. Very few of his cases have become headline news and the PCA himself is hardly a public figure. Whether this is to be regretted or applauded depends on one's perception of his function. The fact that he has unearthed no major scandal even of Crichel Down proportions may be an indication of the quality of the civil service or of the narrowness of his remit. He cannot disclose information obtained for the purpose of his investigation for any other purpose, e.g. to the police (1967 Act, section 11(2)). To change this was said by the then Head of the Civil Service to represent a major change of principle (HC 615, 1977–8, para. 35). He has no power, unlike his counterparts abroad, to make an investigation on his own initiative without a complaint. He is not a trouble-shooter who is asked by the government to investigate major issues of public concern, as again happens elsewhere. There are other mechanisms for this purpose, particularly tribunals of inquiry and select committees which sit in public to hear evidence. He cannot, like the courts, quash a decision or order the payment of damages, though in many cases he has secured *ex gratia* compensation for the complainant. He cannot deal with cases where there is a legal remedy unless he is satisfied that it is not reasonable to expect the complainant to resort to it (1967 Act, section 5(2)). He refused to investigate the cases of haemophiliacs who contracted Aids from blood supplied by the NHS because legal action was being taken (*Guardian*, 31 August 1990). He told Mr Evans, the former editor of *The Times*, who wanted him to investigate its sale to Mr Murdoch which had not been referred to the Monopolies Commission, that this was a political issue which was not within his powers of investigation (*Guardian*, 16 February 1984). When he does get drawn into a politically controversial issue he must, as we have seen, tread the tightrope between maladministration and merits. His main function in such cases, if he does investigate, is to establish the facts impartially, for which he has unparalleled powers. Perhaps the PCA's main importance is that he exists. As he pointed out in one of his reports, 'Those who are inclined to criticize our public service rather freely would do well to consider what it must be like to live in countries where to criticize a great department of state may be to invite imprisonment or worse' (HC 322, 1983–4, para. 1). On the other hand it has been said that the PCA 'was a creature of his time but that time has now largely passed.' (Ryle and Richards, 1988, p. 199) This was said before the publication of the Citizen's Charter and other specific Charters. Though these may have the effect of complaints being settled without resort to the PCA, he remains as a weapon of last resort and the Charters provide him with useful yardsticks for determining maladministration. The PCA himself has singled out the Citizen's Charter as the most important current factor in the publicizing of his office (HC 387, 1992–3, para. 11). Instead of supplanting the PCA, the Citizen's Charter may on the contrary be giving him a new lease of life. The government's Code of Practice on Open Government may have the same effect and has already led to a substantial increase in his funding.

ACCOUNTABILITY TO PARLIAMENT

It could be said that there is not one ombudsman but 651, in that every MP acts as one, or 25000 if one includes local councillors who perform similar functions in relation to local authorities. It has been estimated that MPs take up about a hundred thousand cases with ministers annually (HC 615, 1977–8, para. 6). As we have seen, only a very small proportion (less than 1 per cent) are referred to the PCA for investigation. Most MPs try to get the problems of their constituents solved by their own efforts and only refer cases which are too difficult for them or in order to placate their constituents. It has been suggested that it might be desirable if the citizen could ask the PCA directly to investigate, if he is dissatisfied with the ultimate response from his MP but this has been rejected by the Select Committee (HC 33-I, 1993–4, para. 77). The MP will normally first write a letter to the relevant authority. If correspondence does not lead to a solution he can then ask a parliamentary question. There are certain restrictions on the asking of questions. Ministers can only be asked about matters which fall within the sphere of their responsibility. This has caused problems in relation to the nationalized industries. Under the nationalization legislation ministers only have certain powers and are not responsible for day-to-day matters. Even where questions of detail are technically in order, e.g. under the power to obtain information from the boards, a minister can refuse to answer and thus prevent the question being asked again for a period of time. The problem of asking questions on detail has been circumvented by phrasing the question in terms of asking the minister to give a general direction about the issue at hand, but even this bars questions about particular complaints. Ministers can always deflect the question as falling within the responsibility of the board if it is on a day-to-day matter. When ministers said that they would not vote their shareholding in privatized companies such as British Aerospace, they were told that they could not disclaim responsibility for a stake which they still owned then and had the power to use (HC Deb., vol. 974, col. 70, 19 November 1979). The Westland affair shows that they can certainly not disclaim responsibility for interventions which they do in fact make, provided, of course, that this becomes known. The same rules apply to other quangos over which the minister retains limited powers. MPs may also raise grievances on the adjournment debates at the end of each day's sitting and on the other days set aside for backbenchers, e.g. debates following the passage of the annual Appropriation Bills and the debates on the adjournment of the House for a specified period such as at Christmas.

Financial accountability to Parliament is through the Comptroller and Auditor General (C & AG) who reports to the Public Accounts Committee. The C & AG audits the accounts of government departments and some quangos and is concerned not just with whether money has been spent legally, i.e. in accordance with the Appropriation Act, but whether it has been used economically and efficiently, though he may not question the merits of government policy. On the basis of his reports the Public Accounts Committee questions officials from the Department and in particular the Permanent Secretary who is personally accountable for the expenditure of public money. The political responsibility of the minister is, however, paramount, so that if the Permanent Secretary considers a minister's decision financially irregular or imprudent he must place his objection on record but in the last resort carry out the minister's instructions (HC 393, 1971–2, Q. 133). This is what happened in the case of the Pergau dam project in Malaysia for which aid was provided by the government in spite of the objection of the

Permanent Secretary (HC 155, 1993–4). Such disagreements must now be reported to the C & AG without delay (Cm 2602, 1994).

Governments of both political parties have always resisted allowing the C & AG access to the accounts of the nationalized industries because they argue that this would hinder their freedom to act as commercial bodies. As we have seen, this freedom is much hampered already by ministerial control and it is the desire to preserve accountability to ministers and through them to Parliament which is probably the real stumbling block to granting the C & AG access to the accounts. Similarly, he has no access to the accounts of limited companies in which the government owns some or all of the shares or to whom it gives subsidies. Where public money has been lost, as in the case of the De Lorean car firm in Northern Ireland, he has no access to the accounts of the company, but only to those of the government department, whom he and the Public Accounts Committee can criticize for not monitoring the firm sufficiently (HC 127, 1983–4). Again accountability is through the minister and not directly to Parliament. The select committees which oversee government departments also monitor the nationalized industries but such examinations, unlike those of the Public Accounts Committee, are not based on detailed investigation of the accounts of the departments. The Public Accounts Committee has recently issued an unprecedented report on 'The Proper Conduct of Public Business' (HC 154, 1993–4) following a number of their reports exposing waste and improper expenditure of large sums of money by departments and other public bodies. The Committee warned against public sector values being neglected in the effort to maximise economy and efficiency and requested powers for the C & AG to examine all quangos which receive the greater part of their income from central government funds.

In contrast the accounts of local authorities are audited by auditors appointed by the Audit Commission, a body set up by the Local Government Finance Act 1982. Before that date they were appointed by the minister. The auditor can apply to the court for a declaration that the expenditure of a local authority was unlawful (section 19). In view of the principles applied by the courts to local authorities, such an issue may be highly politically controversial, with the courts declaring unlawful expenditure for which councillors had a mandate from the electorate. Even more controversial is the power to order councillors to repay the money so spent or wrongfully lost and to disqualify them from office, as happened in Liverpool and Lambeth as a result of rebellion over setting a rate in 1985. This gives rise to a conflict between legal and political responsibility which is avoided at the level of central government. Most recently, political controversy has centred on Westminster City Council's policy of selling council properties which the auditor has provisionally found to be for the electoral advantage of the majority party and, therefore, unlawful. He similarly found that certain councillors and officers were guilty of wilful misconduct, that they should be ordered to repay over £20 million and the councillors concerned be disqualified. If the auditor after hearing representations upholds these findings, it will be for the court to finally determine these charges of unprecedented gravity.

None of the mechanisms of control and accountability so far examined involves those who are directly affected by the decisions. The consumer councils of the nationalized industries and the community health councils in the National Health Service do have this function of representing the consumer interest. They have now been overshadowed by the Citizen's Charter initiative which has as its goal efficiency through setting and monitoring standards for public services and redress and compensation for the citizen through complaints machinery. Above all competition is to be the prime instrument of efficiency. The Charter sees the citizen as a consumer not as a participant in decision-making, though it does pay lip-service to consultation. Instead, opting-out as in education and housing, takes the place of participation, and privatization substitutes the market for democratic decision-making. It thereby empowers the strong rather than protects the weak.

CIVIL LIBERTIES
AND A BILL OF RIGHTS

Dicey (1885, p. 195) gave as his third meaning of the Rule of Law, 'that the constitution is pervaded by the rule of law on the ground that the general principles of the constitution (as, for example, the right to personal liberty, or the right of public meeting) are with us the result of judicial decisions determining the rights of private persons in particular cases brought before the courts; whereas under many foreign constitutions the security (such as it is) given to the rights of individuals results, or appears to result, from the general principles of the constitution.' What Dicey regarded as the strength of the constitution so far as civil liberties were concerned is now criticized as one of its weaknesses and has given rise to the call for the enactment of a Bill of Rights modelled on the European Convention for the Protection of Human Rights and Fundamental Freedoms. In order to see how this *volte face* has come about, we will examine how the civil liberties mentioned by Dicey are protected under English law and how they would be safeguarded if a Bill of Rights enacting the European Convention on Human Rights were passed.

PERSONAL LIBERTY

Under this heading are usually included freedom from unlawful arrest and detention and unlawful search of one's person or premises and the seizure of one's property. It is no longer true to say as Dicey did that the rights of the individual in this area are the result of judicial decisions because the Police and Criminal

Evidence Act 1984 now embodies the law on this subject and judicial decisions will now have to interpret the Act and the codes made under it rather than follow previous decisions. It is to this Act, therefore, that we must look for the powers of the police to arrest and detain individuals, to search their person and premises and to seize property. The Act and judicial decisions lay down the limitations on personal liberty, they do not state the rights of the individual. This is the crucial difference from the European Convention on Human Rights. The rights in English law are implicit, it is the limitations of those rights which must be authorized by law. Dicey saw this as an important element of the rule of law, first because the focus is on the remedy by which the rights are safeguarded rather than the rights themselves. He took as his example the remedy of habeas corpus. Historically this was of profound significance but, though the right to apply for habeas corpus is expressly saved by the 1984 Act (section 51(d)), its scope is subject to the provisions of that Act. Secondly, Dicey pointed out that constitutions containing declarations of rights may be suspended and, similarly, the European Convention on Human Rights (except for certain articles) can be derogated from in time of war or other public emergency threatening the life of the nation (article 15). On the other hand, the rights of the individual in Britain cannot be abrogated by a stroke of the pen, though an individual remedy such as habeas corpus has been suspended in time of war or emergency.

However, virtually the same result as the suspension of constitutional rights can come about by an Act of Parliament giving wide powers to the government in time of war or emergency to make regulations to secure the public safety and defence of the realm or the supply and distribution of the necessities of life. In both World Wars the government made regulations under these Acts empowering it to detain persons whom it reasonably believed to be of hostile origin and associations, which in effect deprived such persons of the right to habeas corpus (*Liversidge v. Anderson*, 1942). It is, therefore, the substantive law which limits the freedom of the individual and the remedies by which he can protect his freedom which determine the extent of his liberty. The extent to which these would be affected by the enactment of a Bill of Rights will be considered later.

Arrest and detention

The Police and Criminal Evidence Act 1984 extended the powers of the police to arrest suspects. The power of summary arrest by a police constable applied to reasonable suspicion of an offence punishable with imprisonment for five years (arrestable offences) and in addition to a number of less serious offences where there were specific statutory provisions for arrest. There was also a common law power of arrest for breach of the peace. The Act has widened the category of arrestable offences by adding certain offences which are not punishable with five years' imprisonment (section 24). But more importantly it now gives a power of summary arrest in the case of *any* offence provided certain conditions are satisfied. These are concerned either with the inability to ascertain the correct name or a satisfactory address of the suspect so that it will be impracticable to bring the person before a court by issuing a summons, or with the prevention of serious mischief such as physical injury to himself or others or loss or damage to property. But the latter grounds also include preventing the commission of an offence against public decency and obstruction of the highway, which gives the police a wide discretion (section 25). The provisions in the Act are peppered with the phrase 'has reasonable grounds' for suspecting or doubting or believing. The reasonableness of the grounds can only be tested afterwards by an action for damages for false imprisonment. Similarly, a person must be told both that he is under arrest and the grounds for his arrest; the arrest is not lawful otherwise (section 28). But again this can only be tested afterwards in an action for damages. Persons who are voluntarily helping the police with their inquiries are free to leave unless arrested (section 29) but there are no provisions for telling persons this except at the stage when they are suspected of an offence (Code C: para. 3.15).

The use of powers of arrest varies greatly between police forces.

In *Mohammed-Holgate v. Duke* (1984), an action for wrongful arrest, it was argued that it was unlawful to arrest someone, even if he was reasonably suspected of an arrestable offence, if he was only arrested so that greater pressure could be put on him to confess than if he were interviewed without being arrested. The House of Lords held that, since the police officer had a discretion whether to arrest, once he had reasonable grounds for suspecting an arrestable offence, the exercise of his discretion could not be questioned except on grounds of irrationality (see Chapter 4). This case sanctioned the power of the police to arrest and detain suspects for questioning, provided that there was a power to arrest, before this was explicitly enshrined in the 1984 Act, section 37.

It is now recognized that the primary purpose of detaining a person in police custody after arrest is to obtain from him or through him sufficient evidence to charge him with an offence. The Act and the code made under it are an attempt to hold the balance between giving the police powers to hold the suspect and question him and safeguarding the rights of the individual. Whether the balance is tipped too far in one direction or the other is a matter of judgement that can only be reached after examining the provisions. There is much dispute whether the provisions increased the powers of the police before the Act but the answer is inconclusive because the powers were so uncertain, which was one of the main reasons for passing the Act. The Act and the code are a mixture of police powers and safeguards for the individual, the crucial issue is the extent to which the safeguards are enforceable.

Where the police do not have sufficient evidence to charge the arrested person they may detain him for questioning for up to twenty-four hours with reviews by a superior officer after six hours and nine hours thereafter. At the end of that period he must either be charged with an offence or released (section 41). However, in the case of a serious arrestable offence which is rather widely defined in the Act (section 116), the period of detention can be extended up to thirty-six hours and this can be extended by a magistrates' court for two further periods of up to thirty-six hours to a maximum of ninety-six hours (sections 42–44). This maximum period is longer than that allowed by any common law country but it must be set against the statistics obtained by the Royal Commission on Criminal Procedure (Cmnd 8092, 1981, para. 3.96) that 75 per cent of all suspects are dealt with in six hours and 95 per cent within twenty-four hours; only 0.4 per cent were found to have been held for seventy-two hours or more. A study done since the Act confirms these figures: 76% of detainees were dealt with within 6 hours, less than 1% were detained more than 24 hours and warrants for further detention beyond 36 hours were sought in only 0.2% of cases (Zander, 1990 p. 91). The limits on detention can be enforced by habeas corpus if the practical problems of making an application for the writ can be overcome and an action for damages for wrongful detention could be brought afterwards. The remedies to enforce the other safeguards are not so clear.

When a person is arrested he is given into the charge of a custody officer, who must be of the rank of sergeant or above and who is responsible for ensuring that persons in detention are treated in accordance with the Act and the code made under it (sections 36 and 39) and that a custody record is kept for each person in accordance with the provisions of the Act and the code which lay down what must be recorded, when and by whom. This is to ensure that the procedures laid down are followed correctly and that the safeguards for the treatment of individuals are being observed. But failure to observe these provisions would not make the detention unlawful. Failure to observe the Act or the code renders the police officer liable to disciplinary proceedings (section 67) but there is no independent investigation of complaints against the police, though the Act establishes an independent body, the Police Complaints Authority, to supervise the investigation of complaints (Part IX). There are, however, other safeguards in the Act and the code.

The Act (section 56) gives a person detained in custody the right on request to have someone of his choice informed that he is being detained. This right can be delayed for up to thirty-six hours in the case of a person detained for a serious arrestable offence if there are reasonable grounds for fearing that evidence will be interfered with or other suspects will be alerted. Under the code he must be informed of this right. More importantly the Act (section 58) gives a right to a detained person to consult a solicitor privately on request. Again this right may be delayed for up to thirty-six hours for the same reasons, and again under the code he must be informed of this right. Studies done for the Royal Commission indicated that before the Act, when the right was not statutory, few suspects asked to see a solicitor and most seem to have been refused their request, but they also found that few police forces took adequate steps to make suspects aware of their rights (Cmnd 8092, 1981, para. 4.83). Perhaps the most important change made by the Act is the extension of the duty solicitor scheme to police stations, so that free legal advice will be available round the clock to suspects. Under the code a person may not be interviewed until he has received legal advice, where he has requested it, except where the thirty-six-hour delay applies or he has agreed in writing or where it would unreasonably delay the investigation, which gives further discretion to the police. The solicitor must also be allowed to be present at the interview. Arguably the most important safeguard for suspects contained in the Act are in Section 60 which lays a duty on the Home Secretary to require interviews with suspects to be tape-recorded. In pursuance of this section the Home Secretary issued a code of practice on tape-recording in 1988 and tape-recording of interviews in the case of offences triable by jury was made compulsory from 1 January 1992.

With these safeguards in place it is tempting to ask why it was found necessary to set up another Royal Commission on Criminal Justice in 1991 only ten years after the report of the previous one, whose recommendations gave rise to the 1984 Act. The answer lies in the series of miscarriages of justice which came to light from the late 1980s onwards of which the Maguire 7, the Guildford 4 and the Birmingham 6 were the most prominent. These have been followed by a series of other miscarriages of justice such as the Tottenham 3, the Cardiff 3, the Judith Ward case and the Stefan Kiszko case. Some of these cases but not all predated the safeguards introduced by the 1984 Act. A number of the cases involved terrorism to which even now the same safeguards would not apply. What are the defects in the 1984 Act exposed by these cases and others and to what extent would they be cured by the recommendations of the Royal Commission (Cm 2263, 1993)?

The problem starts at the interview stage if the safeguards are not observed. A research study for the Royal Commission found that only one in four suspects who nominated a firm of solicitors got a qualified solicitor (Cm 2263, Ch. 3, para. 57). In only 32% of cases do suspects request a solicitor (ibid., para. 46) and in only 1% was access delayed under s 58 (Zander, 1990, p. 122). That access may be wrongly delayed is clear from the cases which have come before the courts (see below). Similarly, the tape-recording of interviews did not prevent the brow-beating of the Cardiff 3 (*Guardian*, 17 December 1992) or the obtaining of a confession before the tape-recorder is switched on or in a police car before the suspect has reached the police station.

The key to these problems lies in the sanctions for enforcing the safeguards contained in the Act. Since the questioning of suspects is designed to obtain evidence from them it is the admissibility of such evidence, where the Act or the codes have been breached, that is crucial. The Act provides that a confession is inadmissible where it was obtained by oppression or where anything was said or done which was likely to render it unreliable (section 76). In addition evidence may be excluded where it appears, having regard to all the circumstances, including the way it was obtained, it would have such an adverse effect on the fairness of the proceedings that the court should not admit it (section 78). It has been held in *R. v. Samuel* (1988) that wrongful denial of access to a solicitor did fall within Section 78 so as to render the confession inadmissible, though in a later case the court held the confession admissible, where the defendant had stated in evidence that he knew his rights and, therefore, the presence of the solicitor was not crucial (*R. v. Alladice*, 1988). There have been a plethora of decisions since the Act determining when breaches of the Act rendered confessions inadmissible.

Many of the miscarriages of justice turned on tainted confessions which were admitted at the trials and were sometimes the only evidence. Two possible remedies have been rejected by successive Royal Commissions. The first, to adopt the American exclusionary rule which renders inadmissible illegally obtained evidence was rejected in 1981. The second, to make corroboration of confessions essential was rejected in 1993 (Cm 2263, Chapter 4), though only by a majority.

The reverse case where parents who refused to answer any questions about the death of their baby were not prosecuted because of the absence of any independent witnesses (*Guardian*, 25 February 1993) raises equally fundamental questions about our criminal justice system. It calls into question the right to silence, i.e. the rule which prohibits the refusal to answer questions by the police to be used to infer guilt or to be commented on adversely at the trial. Both Royal Commissions have recommended the retention of this fundamental right against self-incrimination, but the government rejected this recommendation in 1993. The Criminal Justice and Public Order Bill 1994 (Part III) allows the court or jury to draw such inferences as appear proper from the accused's failure, when questioned by the police, to mention a fact on which he relies in his defence which he could reasonably have been expected to mention. The same inferences may be drawn from his failure to give evidence at his trial and from the failure of an arrested person to account for objects, substances or marks, or his presence at a particular place. These provisions are modelled on those already in force in Northern Ireland. While it is hoped that they will lead to the conviction of more guilty defendants, the fear is that they are likely to lead to the conviction of more innocent but vulnerable persons. The Royal Commission was concerned with the possibility of more miscarriages of justice, the government with the obtaining of more convictions. The House of Lords' attempt to find a compromise solution to allow inferences to be drawn from silence but provide better safeguards for those being questioned, resulted in an amendment to make a caution obligatory before questioning by the police but an amendment which would have required the questioning to take place in a police station with the attendant safeguards was defeated (HL Deb., vol. 556, col. 1386 seq., 7 July 1994).

No safeguards can be foolproof against the fabrication of evidence by the police which was responsible for some of the miscarriages of justice, particularly those in which the West Midlands CID was involved which was disbanded. The only remedy in such cases must be retrospective, namely the quashing of the conviction and prosecution or disciplinary proceedings and an action for damages against the police. In the case of the Guildford 4, though the convictions were quashed, the three police officers who were prosecuted were acquitted. In the case of the Birmingham 6, the judge ordered the prosecution to be dropped because the intensity of media publicity made it impossible to have a fair trial. The double jeopardy rule has prevented disciplinary proceedings for an offence for which a prosecution has been brought. This rule has been abolished by the Police and Magistrates' Courts Act 1994.

It is not just the police but the whole of our criminal justice system which has been called into question by the mounting number of miscarriages of justice. The Royal Commission did not recommend any fundamental reforms such as a change from our adversarial system, where the trial is a battle between prosecution and defence before an impartial tribunal, to an inquisitorial system where the judge plays an active part in the investigation and at the trial in the search for truth. On the other hand, the curtailment of the right to silence is likely to increase miscarriages of justice, though the Criminal Cases Review Authority which was proposed by the Royal Commission (chapter 11) and is now subject to consultation, may ensure that more miscarriages are corrected after they have taken place.

Stop and search power

There is power under the Act (Part I) to stop and search persons and vehicles in a public place on reasonable suspicion of finding stolen goods or offensive weapons. This power previously existed only in certain areas of the country which had obtained special legislation in private Acts of Parliament. It is a very controversial power which has had particular impact on some sections of the community such as young black people and which Lord Scarman pinpointed as a contributory factor in sparking off the Brixton disorders (Cmnd 8427, 1981, para. 3.27). The code of practice on stop and search powers now lays down guidance on what does and does not constitute reasonable suspicion and states explicitly that colour or style of dress can never by themselves be grounds for reasonable suspicion. But breach of the code is not a crime nor does it give rise to an action for damages by itself, though it must be taken into account in any proceedings to which it is relevant (section 67), which would be an action for assault where the stop and search was unlawful. The use by the police of stop and search powers has increased dramatically in recent years and they seem to be used by the police for information gathering, as only 15% of those searched are arrested. Young blacks are still far more likely to be stopped than the average person. These figures were seen as extremely disturbing by civil liberties groups (*Guardian*, 4 July 1992). There is a new power in the Criminal Justice and Public Order Bill 1994 to stop and search persons and vehicles for a maximum of 30 hours where the police reasonably believe serious violence may take place in an area.

Search and seizure

The other main police power under the Act is to enter and search premises and seize property. From a historical point of view this is perhaps the greatest infringement of individual liberty because the great constitutional case proclaimed in ringing tones the principle that an Englishman's home is his castle, 'The great end, for which men entered into society, was to secure their property' (*Entick v. Carrington*, 1765). This eighteenth-century case decided that it was illegal for the Home Secretary to issue a warrant authorizing entry of a person's house to search for and seize his papers to find evidence of seditious libel. Since that case was decided, the power to search for evidence of an offence or for unlawful articles was conferred by a number of statutes, but there were glaring gaps such as the lack of a power to issue a search warrant to find evidence in the case of murder. This was highlighted in the case of *Ghani v. Jones* (1970) where the police managed to obtain the passports and letters from persons they suspected of being implicated in a murder but were ordered to hand them back by Lord Denning because they had not shown reasonable grounds for believing that the plaintiffs were implicated in the crime or that the documents were material evidence to prove commission of the crime. In that case Lord Denning laid down sweeping propositions of law about search and seizure of property for which there was little authority. This confused and haphazard state of the law cried out for reform which is now embodied in the 1984 Act.

The Act for the first time gave a general power to the police to obtain a warrant from a magistrate to enter premises and to search for evidence where they have reasonable grounds to believe that a serious arrestable offence has been committed and that this was the only practicable way to obtain the evidence (section 8). The premises may be those of a third party who is not suspected of any offence. When the Bill was first published there was an outcry from the caring professions, e.g. doctors and social workers, who feared the possibility of their confidential records being ransacked to find evidence of a crime. As a result the second Bill was substantially modified so as to exclude from its ambit altogether confidential personal records as well as confidential journalistic material in addition to communications between a client and his legal adviser which had been previously excluded. Other confidential or journalistic material can only be searched for by obtaining an order from a circuit judge (section 9).

These powers have been used extensively to order the media, who cover demonstrations where disturbances take place, to hand over to the police photographs or film to help with the identification of suspects. The media have unsuccessfully objected to such orders because of the danger of journalists being attacked by demonstrators to avoid detection. Under the Prevention of Terrorism Act 1989 (Schedule 7) there are even more draconian powers under which orders can be made to hand over material which would be excluded under the 1984 Act, namely confidential journalistic material such as the sources from which information was obtained. Channel 4 were found guilty of contempt of court for refusing to comply with such an order, which would have endangered the life of an informant whose identity was not disclosed in a programme about terrorism in Northern Ireland (*Guardian*, 1 August 1992).

No warrant or order is necessary to search the premises in which a person was arrested (section 32) for evidence relating to the offence or to search the premises occupied by someone arrested for an arrestable offence after his arrest (section 18) for evidence relating to that offence or a related or similar offence. Once lawfully on the premises, the police may take anything which they reasonably believe is evidence of any offence whatsoever in order to prevent the evidence being lost or destroyed (section 19). These provisions put into statutory form some of the most controversial statements made by Lord Denning in *Ghani v. Jones* (1970) and even go beyond them. They encourage the police to go on fishing expeditions, looking for evidence which is not within the warrant or is not connected with the offence for which a person is arrested. Though such searches may be illegal under the provisions of the Act (sections 16(8), 18(3) and 32(3)), evidence so found would not be inadmissible unless it fell within the provision for the exclusion of unfair evidence (section 78). The Royal Commission would have excluded evidence obtained by an illegal search (Cmnd 8092, 1981, para. 3.49) to minimize fishing expeditions. The possibility of an action for damages after the event against the police and possible disciplinary proceedings are not a sufficient deterrent. The Englishman's castle has let down its drawbridge for the police.

Telephone tapping and surveillance

The police have other means of obtaining evidence of an offence which are subject to even fewer safeguards than is the searching of premises. Telephone tapping was, until April 1986, when the

Interception of Communications Act 1985 came into force, carried out under the authority of a warrant issued by a Secretary of State in accordance with guidelines which had been laid down by him. When the legality of this procedure was challenged in *Malone v. Metropolitan Police Commissioner* (1979) the judge did not follow *Entick v. Carrington* (1765) and hold such warrants illegal because no property right was infringed by telephone tapping. He held that 'it can lawfully be done simply because there is nothing to make it unlawful' (pp. 733–4). The principle, which can be regarded as an important safeguard for the rights of the individual, had a diametrically opposite result here. *Malone* took his case to the European Court of Human Rights (1984) where it was held that the United Kingdom had broken the European Convention on Human Rights, Article 8, under which everyone has the right to respect for his private and family life, his home and his correspondence. The court held that the minimum degree of legal protection to which citizens are entitled under the rule of law in a democratic society was lacking. To comply with the judgement, the Interception of Communications Act 1985 was passed by Parliament. This makes telephone tapping a criminal offence except where it is carried out by consent or under the authority of a warrant issued by the Secretary of State in accordance with the provisions of the Act (section 1). The Act now lays down in broad terms the grounds on which warrants may be issued, their scope and duration and the procedure for issuing them, as well as other safeguards (sections 2–6). A tribunal of lawyers has been set up to whom complaint can be made by someone who thinks his telephone has been tapped, but they can only investigate whether there has been a warrant issued and whether this complies with the Act (section 7). They cannot investigate illegal tapping without a warrant, for which a prosecution can be brought only with the consent of the Director of Public Prosecutions. The decisions of the tribunal cannot be challenged in any court (section 7) nor can any proceedings be brought before a court challenging the legality of a warrant or the legality of telephone tapping except where there is a prosecution for illegal tapping (section 9). It would, therefore, now be impossible for someone in the position of *Malone* to bring his case before a court. It was, however, possible for the Campaign for Nuclear Disarmament (CND) to challenge the legality of a warrant allegedly issued by the Home Secretary to tap the phone of its vice-president before the Act came into force. The judge rejected the application because he held that the warrant had been lawfully issued on grounds of national security. He held that he could review the case even though it involved a question of national security and went on to hold that in accordance with the doctrine of legitimate expectation (see Chapter 4) ministers were bound by their own guidelines. (*R. v. Secretary of State for the Home Department ex parte Ruddock*, 1987).

The 1985 Act was used as the model when the Security Service (MI5) and the Intelligence Service (MI6) and GCHQ were placed on a statutory footing by the Security Service Act 1989 and the Intelligence Services Act 1994. The Services were given statutory authority to apply for warrants from the relevant Secretary of State to enter or interfere with property, if he thinks it is necessary to obtain information for the discharge of their functions. These are defined as the protection of national security and in particular its protection against threats from espionage, terrorism and actions intended to overthrow parliamentary democracy by political, industrial or violent means and to safeguard the economic well-being of the UK against threats from outside Britain (MI5) and to obtain information about persons outside the UK in the interests of national security (MI6). The exercise of the Secretary of State's power to issue warrants is overseen under each Act by a Commissioner, who must be or have been a judge, and a Tribunal consisting of lawyers to whom complaints can be made about alleged interference with property. Such complaints must be referred to the relevant Commissioner who has to investigate whether a warrant has been issued and, if it has, whether it has been properly issued. A person may also complain to the relevant Tribunal if he thinks inquiries are being made about him by one of the Services and the Tribunal can determine, whether, if this is the case, they had reasonable grounds for doing so. If the finding is in favour of the complainant they can order the inquiries to cease or quash a warrant and direct the Secretary of State to pay compensation.

No determination has been made in favour of the complainant by either the Tribunal or the Commissioner overseeing MI5. In the 1993 report of the Commissioner it is stated specifically that in his opinion no unlawful interference with property is carried out without the issue of a warrant, though he adds the rider that, as he cannot review the operations of the Service itself, as distinct from the issue of a warrant by the Home Secretary, he cannot give a categorical assurance (Cm 2174, 1993). His counterpart, the Commissioner under the Interception of Communications Act, made the point more forcefully that stories in the newspapers alleging interception by the security services 'are, in my experience without exception, false' (Cm 2173, 1993). These statements were no doubt intended to counter allegations about the bugging of telephone conversations of members of the royal family. They would carry more conviction if there were more open accountability for the security services.

The Home Affairs Committee recommended that the Security Service (MI5) should be brought within its terms of reference so that it could scrutinize its general policy and the value-for-money of expenditure by the Service but not operational matters. It also drew attention to much more open oversight of the security services in other countries (HC 265, 1992–3). The government has responded by provision in the Intelligence Services Act 1994 (Section 10) for a Committee of nine members drawn from both Houses of Parliament to examine the expenditure, administration and policy of MI5, MI6 and GCHQ. They are to be appointed by the Prime Minister after consultation with the Leader of the Opposition and can be dismissed by him at any time. Unlike other Parliamentary Committees it will report annually to the Prime Minister rather than directly to Parliament. Though the Prime Minister has to lay the report before Parliament, he can exclude from the report matter which he thinks would be prejudicial to the discharge of the functions of the security services. Also the Committee will not be able to obtain information defined as sensitive in the Act, e.g. operational matters, which neither the Secretary of State nor the director of one of the security services considers it safe to disclose. Further the Secretary of State can prevent disclosure on the same grounds on which he withholds information from departmental Select Committees of the House of Commons (supra. p.35) but not on grounds of national security alone. The Committee will not have the usual power of departmental committees to call for evidence and will have no staff of its own. Whether such a committee can restore faith in the security services is open to question.

FREEDOM OF SPEECH AND PUBLIC ASSEMBLY

Dicey said of the right to free speech, 'Freedom of discussion is then, in England, little else than the right to write or say anything which a jury consisting of twelve shopkeepers think it expedient should be said or written' (p. 246). He was, of course, referring to the law of libel. But Dicey was mainly concerned in his discussion of freedom of speech to contrast freedom of the press in Britain with that in France. His basic argument was that the press in Britain was subject to the ordinary law of the land and there was no special press law providing for censorship or giving the press special privileges. In essence that is true today, though, as we have seen, journalistic material is given a special status under the Police and Criminal Evidence Act 1984. Journalists, having obtained these special provisions, later had second thoughts for the reasons given by Dicey, because it singled them out for special treatment.

There are many other legal restrictions on freedom of speech both at common law and by statute apart from the law of libel. Increasingly today individuals want to exercise freedom of speech not in isolation but together with their fellow citizens in marches and demonstrations. This is when the right has to be balanced against public order and the rights of other citizens to go about their business. Mass picketing during industrial disputes raises similar issues. The law which holds the balance between these conflicting freedoms is now mostly contained in the Public Order

Act 1986 and the Criminal Justice and Public Order Bill 1994 (Part V) which embody in statutory form with some modifications the common law public order offences of riot, rout, unlawful assembly and affray and also re-enact and amend the statutory offences dealing with processions and public assemblies previously contained in the Public Order Act 1936.

The Public Order Act 1986, like the Police and Criminal Evidence Act 1984, contains restrictions on the freedom of the individual; it does not state the right of the individual to assemble peacefully. An unsuccessful attempt was made in the House of Lords (HL Deb., vol. 479, col. 436, 24 July 1986) to include a clause in the Bill stating that persons shall be lawfully entitled peacefully to demonstrate or peacefully to hold assemblies. It was rejected by the government partly for the reason that it is a fundamental precept of English law that we are all free to do anything not prohibited by law.

The problem of balancing the freedom to assemble against public order is not a new one. It is epitomized in the old case of *Beatty v. Gillbanks* (1882) where the Salvation Army in Weston-super-Mare were wont to march on a Sunday with a band and banners flying. They were opposed by the Skeleton Army who were antagonistic to their views. Fights ensued and the Salvation Army were told not to march. When they persisted despite being asked by the police to disperse, their leaders were arrested and charged with unlawful assembly. On appeal they were held not guilty because the disturbance of the peace was the fault of their opponents and had not been caused by them. This case was distinguished in the later case of *Duncan v. Jones* (1936) where the facts are closer to the problems of our times. Mrs Duncan wanted to hold a meeting to protest about a repressive Bill, then before Parliament, outside a training centre for the unemployed. On a previous occasion a meeting in the same place addressed by Mrs Duncan had led to disturbances in the training centre. The police asked her to hold the meeting a little distance away; she refused and was arrested. She was convicted of obstructing the police in the execution of their duty. Much ink has been spilt over the attempt to reconcile these cases. This is now merely a matter of historical significance. Under the Public Order Act 1986 the Salvation Army would not be guilty of the offence of violent disorder (section 2) because they did not use or threaten violence nor would they be guilty of the offence of using threatening, abusive or insulting words or behaviour which is intended or likely to cause fear of or to provoke immediate violence (section 4). The law on obstruction of the police has not been changed. More importantly, what the cases illustrate is the eternal difficulty of reconciling freedom of speech and meeting with public order and in consequence the problems of making and applying laws to hold the balance between them. This is particularly true at times of political and economic unrest and it is no coincidence that the first Public Order Act in 1936 was passed because of disturbances resulting from fascist marches and that the second Public Order Act was passed in 1986 in the aftermath of inner-city riots, the mass picketing during the miners' strike and mass demonstrations by protest groups. Part V of the 1994 Bill is concerned with hunt saboteurs and mass protests as well as 'raves', squatters and New Age Travellers.

In view of this it is not surprising that the legislation tips the balance further in favour of public order and against freedom of meeting. The government recognized in its White Paper preceding the 1986 Act (Cmnd 9510, 1985, para. 1.9) that tightening of the law cannot by itself prevent all disorder and that after disorder has broken out the problem is not a shortage of legal powers but enforcement. This is a matter of practical policing and raises questions of equipment and tactics. More importantly, in the case of large-scale disorders, such as the Brixton and other inner-city riots, it raises questions of social policy, particularly towards ethnic minorities, as Lord Scarman stressed in his historic report on the Brixton disorders (Cmnd 8427, 1981, Part VI). It is in the provisions which give the police powers to prevent disorder that the Public Order Act 1986 tips the balance further against the freedom of speech and assembly.

One of the main new provisions in the Act is section 11 which makes it an offence for those organizing a procession to demonstrate for or against a cause or to publicize it or to mark or commemorate an event, not to give six days' advance notice to the police unless this is not reasonably practicable, as in the case of spontaneous demonstrations. This provision is new only in the sense that it applies to the whole country, whereas previous provisions for advance notice only applied in certain areas. It has been argued that the provision is unnecessary as the police usually know in advance about major processions, though this is not so in a minority of cases. The giving of notice is seen as providing a trigger for discussions between the police and the organizers about the manner of conducting the march so as to make the exercise of the statutory powers regulating it unnecessary. On the other hand, where there was no prior knowledge of the march by the police, it would alert them in time to use their powers. It is interesting that a similar provision for static demonstrations and meetings was ruled out by the government for the purely practical reason of generating too much work for the police.

One of the most controversial provisions in the Act was the extension of the powers of the police to impose conditions on a procession (section 12). Though the formal power to give directions imposing conditions which existed under the 1936 Act was rarely used, the existence of the power enables the police to negotiate with the organizers, and the wider the power, the stronger is the bargaining position of the police. The main extension has been in the tests which have to be satisfied before conditions can be imposed. Under the 1936 Act the chief officer of police had to have reasonable grounds for apprehending that the procession might result in serious public disorder. To this the 1986 Act adds reasonable belief of serious damage to property, serious disruption to the life of the community or that the purpose of the organizers is the intimidation of others. These tests widen the power greatly and if used to the full extent could bring almost any large procession within its scope. In theory the exercise of the power could be tested in the courts but in practice the courts have been reluctant to substitute their judgement for that of the police in this area. The conditions which may be imposed are those which appear necessary to the chief constable to prevent disorder, damage, disruption or intimidation, including prescribing the route. It is also now made explicit that conditions can be imposed during the march as well as in advance and the power can then be exercised by the most senior police officer present who could be of junior rank. Failure to comply with a condition knowingly is an offence for the organizers and those taking part and they may be summarily arrested.

Even more controversial has been the extension of this power to impose conditions to public assemblies (section 14). The criteria for the exercise of the power are the same as for processions, and conditions may be imposed as to the place, the duration and the number of persons who may take part. This provision will for the first time give the police a specific statutory power to limit the number of pickets and where they stand, provided that one of the criteria for imposing conditions applies, which in the case of mass picketing would almost certainly be the case. Failure to comply knowingly will be an offence for which one can be summarily arrested. If the powers under this provision were used to the full extent they would enable the police to exercise control over almost any sizeable demonstration. To fall within the provisions the assembly must be of twenty or more people and be held in a public place which is wholly or partly open to the air. This definition carefully excludes private land to which the public is not admitted, and much pressure was brought on the government to extend the Act to trespassers on private land. At a late stage in the Bill the government finally succumbed to pressure and tabled an amendment to give the police power to direct trespassers to leave land if they reasonably believe that two or more trespassers intend to reside there for any period, that the occupier has taken reasonable steps to get them to leave and that they have caused damage to property or used threatening words or behaviour or have brought twelve or more vehicles on to the land. Failure to obey such a direction or return within three months is a criminal offence (section 39). This section has been considerably widened by Part V of the 1994 Bill. Not only has the number of vehicles been reduced to six but there is now power for the police to seize and remove vehicles where a direction to leave the land is in force. Also, a local authority can give a direction to leave to anyone residing in a vehicle on a highway or unoccupied land as well as trespassers on occupied land. A magistrates' court can order removal of a vehicle which remains in contravention of such a direction.

These provisions to issue directions to leave land have been used as the model in the 1994 Bill for controlling 'raves', i.e. concerts of 100 or more people in the open air at night which are likely to cause serious distress to local residents, the music being defined as including, 'the emission of a succession of repetitive beats'. Again the police are given the power to seize and remove vehicles or sound equipment where a direction to leave the land is in force and even to stop persons on the way to a 'rave' within five miles of the site and direct them not to proceed. Failure to obey a direction is an offence.

Similarly, the power to issue directions to leave the land can be used against those committing a new offence of aggravated trespass, which is aimed at those who trespass on land in the open air to intimidate, obstruct or disrupt any lawful activity, e.g. hunt saboteurs or motorway protestors. This provision goes furthest towards turning trespass into a criminal offence.

The 1994 Bill also breaks new ground by giving the police power for the first time to apply for a ban on certain assemblies, modelled on the power for banning public processions which has existed since 1936. The assembly must be of at least 20 people trespassing on land in the open air including a highway and either be likely to seriously disrupt the life of the community, or to cause significant damage to land or buildings of historical, architectural, archaeological or scientific importance. The ban cannot exceed four days or an area of more than five miles radius. These provisions are tailor-made to give the police further powers to deal with the annual demonstrations at Stonehenge during the summer solstice. For several years the police have used their powers under section 13 of the Public Order Act 1986 (a re-enactment of the provision in the 1936 Act) to ban processions within a certain radius of the monument. The power can only be used where the chief constable reasonably believes that the power to impose conditions on a procession will not be sufficient to prevent serious public disorder. In exercising this power the chief constable must take into account the mutual aid arrangements whereby he can call on assistance from other police forces. He can then apply to the local authority or in London to the Home Secretary for an order banning all processions or a class of procession for up to three months. The order can only be made with the consent of the Home Secretary both in London and elsewhere. There is no power to ban a specific procession because of the danger that this could lead to accusations of political bias. This does, however, mean that, for example, the National Front can stop all other marches by announcing that they will hold a march which as a result of counter-demonstrations is likely to result in serious public disorder. This has happened on a number of occasions and banning orders increased in the early 1980s. Lord Scarman would have liked a power to ban a specific march if there were reasonable grounds for believing that the march was a threat to public order and likely to stir up racial hatred (Cmnd 8427, 1981, para. 7.48). There is no such provision in the 1986 Act which does, however, make the law relating to incitement to racial hatred more effective by giving for the first time a power of summary arrest in such a case (section 18) and the 1994 Bill added such a power for the offence of distributing racist literature.

The legsilation contains no provision for charging the organizers of a demonstration with the cost of policing it. The practical difficulties involved would be very great, but reconciling freedom of speech with public order can be expensive. The policing of Stonehenge during the summer solstice in 1992 cost £200,000 (*Guardian*, 18 June 1993).

Probably the most important common law power which the police retain is to prevent imminent breaches of the peace and arrest those responsible. This power was greatly extended during the miners' strike when miners were stopped at a road block on the M1 and were arrested when they tried to proceed. Their conviction for obstructing the police was upheld because on the facts the police acted reasonably in forming the opinion that there was a real risk of a breach of the peace in close proximity both in place and time, there being four pits within five miles of the road block (*Moss v. McLachlan, The Times*, 29 November 1984). That this case was hailed as a limitation on police powers shows how much the police had stretched their powers in setting up other road blocks. The road blocks set up during the industrial dispute at the News International plant at Wapping were justified by the police under the Metropolitan Police Act 1839, section 52 which gives power to direct constables to keep order and prevent obstruction in the immediate neighbourhood of places of public resort and when the streets may be thronged or obstructed. The civil law of trespass has also been used to obtain injunctions against demonstrators protesting against the motorway through Twyford Down. On the other hand the civil law of assault and wrongful arrest has been used by protesters to recover damages against the police for their conduct at demonstrations. This can be the most effective vindication of the right to protest peacefully.

A BILL OF RIGHTS

How would the protection of civil liberties be affected if Britain enacted a Bill of Rights based on the European Convention on Human Rights?

Britain is a signatory of this Convention, and individuals such as Malone, who think that their rights under the Convention have been infringed, can bring a petition against the United Kingdom before the European Commission of Human Rights. The Commission may be able to reach a friendly settlement between the parties. If this cannot be achieved, it may refer the case to the European Court of Human Rights consisting of a judge from each country. In future, when amendments to the Convention have been ratified by all member States, the Commission will cease to exist and the Court will become full-time. Normally three judges will decide the admissibility of the petition and seven judges on its merits. The judgements of the Court are binding on countries which have signed the Convention but they cannot be enforced. There have been more petitions against the United

Kingdom and more have been upheld than against any other signatory which allows individual petitions except Italy. They span an enormous range of issues. Apart from the *Malone* case on telephone tapping, they include interrogation methods in Northern Ireland, the closed shop, caning in schools, the immigration rules, the law on homosexuality in Northern Ireland, the abolition of the GLC, the banning of trade unions at GCHQ, the anti-terrorist legislation, the law on contempt, the use of plastic bullets, the rights of prisoners and mental patients, the banning of the book *Spycatcher*, the activities of MI5 and the law on leasehold reform challenged by the Duke of Westminster. Not all these petitions were successful but more than eighty legal provisions have been changed as the result of proceedings under the Convention. British governments have been meticulous in complying with the judgements of the Court, though, as the Interception of Communications Act 1985 shows, this may be the minimum compliance necessary to satisfy the judgement. The procedure for obtaining redress by an individual is slow – it can take five years or more – and legal aid is only available on a limited basis.

Those who support enacting a Bill of Rights into the law of the United Kingdom now include the Labour party as well as the Liberal Democrats, the all-party pressure group Charter 88, the Master of the Rolls and the Lord Chief Justice. On several occasions Bills embodying the European Convention have been passed through the House of Lords, in 1986 a Bill was supported by Lord Scarman. None of these Bills has so far been acceptable to a British government. A Human Rights Bill failed to obtain a second reading in the House of Commons on 6 February 1987 (HC Deb., vol. 109, col. 1288). These Bills raise fundamental constitutional issues.

The first problem that has to be confronted is the extent to which legal force can be given to the Convention when enacted in an Act of Parliament. The most fundamental rule of the constitution, implicit in the sovereignty of Parliament, is that one Parliament cannot bind its successors. It is, therefore, legally impossible to prevent a future Parliament legislating expressly in contravention of an Act which embodies the Convention. In accordance with the strict interpretation of the doctrine of sovereignty, it is even legally impossible to prevent a future Parliament passing legislation which is inconsistent with the rights under the Convention by implication rather than expressly. In 1986, as on a previous Bill in 1978, the Human Rights Bill had to be amended in the House of Lords to comply with this fundamental rule of the constitution. So far as Acts passed before the Human Rights Bill are concerned, it is, however, possible to provide that they shall only be effective insofar as they do not infringe the rights embodied in the Bill. Also, so far as Acts passed after the enacting of the Human Rights Bill are concerned, it is possible to provide that they shall be construed so as not to infringe the rights there set out except where this is unavoidable in order to give effect to such an Act.

Even without enactment the Convention has some legal effect. It has been used in argument in a number of important cases including *Malone* and *Spycatcher*. As the *Malone* case shows, the Convention cannot confer legal rights enforceable in the English courts. However, the Convention is an international treaty and, therefore, falls within the rule of statutory interpretation that a statute or subordinate legislation should be construed, where this is reasonably possible, so as to be consistent with the international obligations of the UK but a treaty cannot override clear statutory provisions. It is, therefore, in cases of ambiguity that the Convention can be called in aid. The courts have refused to apply this rule to a broad discretionary power conferred on the Home Secretary to give directives to the BBC and the Independent Broadcasting Authority not to broadcast any matter specified in the notice. The court held that he was not obliged to conform to the Convention, which gives the right to freedom of expression (Article 10), when issuing a directive about broadcasting interviews with terrorists because this would be tantamount to incorporating the Convention into English law by the back-door (*R. v. Secretary of State for the Home Department ex parte Brind*, 1991).

The Convention may also be resorted to when there is uncertainty in the common law or alternatively the court may declare that English law is the same as the right set out in the Convention. The latter position was adopted by the House of Lords with regard to freedom of speech in the *Spycatcher* case (1988) and was reiterated in *Derbyshire County Council v. Times Newspapers* (1993) where the House of Lords held that a local authority could not sue in libel because this would place an undesirable fetter on freedom of speech. Applying the same principle of freedom of speech, the Court of Appeal decided that large awards of damages for libel should be subject to more searching scrutiny than in the past and that the Court should give proper weight to guidance given by the European Court of Human Rights on the interpretation of Article 10 (*Rantzen v. Mirror Group Newspapers Ltd*, 1993). This is edging closer to an incorporation of the Convention into English law by the back door. It also reverses the traditional position that English law does not lay down rights but only restrictions on the freedom of the individual.

Of more importance than these purely legal issues is the political issue of whether it is desirable that Britain should embody the European Convention into English law rather than merely allow aggrieved individuals to petition under the European Convention. The crucial difference would be that the Convention would be binding on British courts and, therefore, the rights in the Convention would be enforceable in British courts. Whether this is a good thing or not is a highly controversial question on which there are differences of opinion within the judiciary, the political parties and among constitutional lawyers. Basically the argument turns on whether British judges should be involved in interpreting the very broad terms of the Convention embodying highly politically controversial issues, such as the ones that have been decided by the European Court. The fear is that British judges are not skilled in interpreting broad provisions of this nature and that they would either interpret them legalistically or become involved in political decision-making to a far greater extent than is true currently. The independence of the judiciary from political pressure is one of the cornerstones of the constitution embodied in the Act of

Settlement 1701, which provided that judges could only be removed for misbehaviour on an address of both Houses of Parliament. If the judges entered the political arena their impartiality would be much more open to question than at present and governments might be tempted to make political appointments, as is the case with appointments to the Supreme Court in the United States. As we have seen, a British court, unlike the US Supreme Court, would not have the last word in respect of legislation passed by Parliament. Nevertheless the enactment of the European Convention into law would confer considerable political power on an unelected body of persons and constitute an important check on democracy. Whether this is regarded as desirable depends on one's faith in our democratic institutions.

CONCLUSION

'I think that we are the witnesses of the death of democracy in Britain. We are witnessing that death because the House has lost the will to assert its authority as a legislative chamber.' Mr Tony Benn MP.

'The corruption in the apple that has diminished Parliament is that, for too many years, the Government and the Opposition have been satisfied to seek merely acquiescence not consent.' Mr Richard Shepherd MP.

These two statements, one from each side of the House, made during the confidence debate on the Maastricht Treaty (HC Deb., vol. 229, col. 657 and 665, 23 July 1993), encapsulate what is wrong with our democratic institutions. The origin lies in the Glorious Revolution of 1688 embodied in the Bill of Rights 1689 which asserts the sovereignty of Parliament, the cornerstone of our constitution. The Bill of Rights abolished the prerogatives of the Crown to levy taxes and set aside laws and the courts accepted the supremacy of Parliament thus laying the foundation for the elective dictatorship. This did not become apparent until the rise of democracy through the reform of the franchise from 1832 onwards. The Crown now had to choose its ministers from the party who had a majority of seats in the House of Commons. This resulted in the fusion of executive and legislative power which Bagehot (1867) regarded as the efficient secret of the British Constitution. But it was the extension of the franchise, which gave rise to the mass party with its whipped cohorts of MPs, that transformed the balance of power between government and

Parliament and resulted in the elective dictatorship where the government controls Parliament and not Parliament the government. The paradox is that the extension of democracy in Britain has strengthened rather than weakened the government (Amery, 1953).

This is most apparent from our first past the post electoral system which is designed to produce a government with a majority of seats in the House of Commons rather than reflect arithmetically the proportion of votes cast for each party. The unprecedented fourth election victory of the Conservative government in 1992 has raised the spectre of a one-party state with all the consequences that this implies. The most important is the lack of balance or check on power which is inherent in governments alternating in office. It is possible, in spite of all the obstacles under our electoral system for the opposition, that the government will be defeated at the next election, by the electorate voting tactically against the government, in favour of the opposition party most likely to win the seat, rather than for the party they support. Paradoxically this may best be fostered by the opposition parties being seen to be independent of each other but developing convergent policies so that they could work together in a hung Parliament. The electorate might thus bring about the same result as the adoption of a system of proportional representation.

Any power sharing between a major and minority party whether as a result of a hung Parliament or a change in the electoral system gives disproportionate weight to the minority, enabling it to hold the balance of power and even switch its allegiance to another party. This happened in Germany in 1982, when the Free Democratic Party broke away from the Social Democrats and joined the Christian Democrats. The spectacle of the minority holding the majority to ransom is not a good advertisement for democracy, especially if the minority party is an extremist party whether of the right or of the left. This has happened in some countries which have proportional representation. Similarly, in Britain when there is a hung Parliament or the government has a small majority, deals have been struck with minority parties. Labour negotiated the Lib-Lab pact in 1977 when it had lost its majority and the Conservatives with a small majority struck a deal with the Ulster Unionists before the crucial debate on the Social Chapter of the Maastricht Treaty on 22 July 1993. In these circumstances deals also have to be struck within parties to buy off rebellion as happened with the Conservative Euro-sceptics at the time of the 'paving debate' for the Maastricht Treaty on 4 November 1992. Wheeling and dealing is not, therefore, the sole preserve of countries which have proportional representation. It is more a difference of degree than of kind from the position in Britain, where both major parties are in effect coalitions representing a wide spectrum of views and interests which have to be kept together. The difference is that loyalty within a party tends to be stronger than between parties. The hallmark of this strength is the vote of confidence as was most recently illustrated on 23 July 1993.

Is the elective dictatorship the necessary price Britain pays for stable government? This is by no means inevitable: ultimately the issue is one of balance. If MPs asserted themselves, as Mr Benn suggests, the balance of power between the government and Parliament could be redressed. The rebellion of Conservative MPs over the Maastricht Treaty and pit closures shows the influence that can be wielded by a group of government back-benchers, particularly when there is a small majority. In the end they may not have achieved their objective but this was partly because they succumbed to intense whipping and, in the case of the Maastricht Treaty, the use of the ultimate deterrent, i.e. a vote of confidence. On the issue of Maastricht they kept the debate on the Bill going for fifteen months and with regard to pit closures they were placated by a compromise. If MPs more frequently voted in accordance with their consciences and convictions rather than their party, the relationship between the executive and the legislature could be transformed.

This is particularly true in relation to select committees. There are numerous examples of highly critical reports by these committees, often reached unanimously across party lines, which are sunk almost without trace when they reach the floor of the

House. The reports on the Westland affair, pit closures and rail privatization are only the most conspicuous examples. This cannot be altered by adjustments to the committees, it can only be changed by MPs themselves behaving differently. Only in this way can a balance of power between government and Parliament be restored to compensate for a lack of a separation of powers between them.

The House of Lords as presently constituted lacks legitimacy. It can be a thorn in the flesh of the government but it cannot alter the balance of power between the executive and the legislature. Any proposals for reform, which envisage an elected House, have to steer between the twin dangers of a House with a different party political complexion coming into conflict with the Commons or one of the same party which merely duplicates the lower House. A careful delimitation of powers can prevent an elected House of Lords being a rival to the Commons.

The shift in the balance of power between the government and Parliament is seen most starkly when Parliament is by-passed through the use of delegated legislation. Increasingly statutes are becoming skeleton Acts providing wide discretionary powers to ministers to make statutory instruments which are subject to very attenuated parliamentary scrutiny. The new House of Lords committee for the Scrutiny of Delegated Powers is a step towards better monitoring of such provisions but there is much room for the improvement of scrutiny of statutory instruments by standing committees, especially by hearing evidence as already happens in the case of the standing committees scrutinising European legislation. But by far the most important reform would be the exercise of self-restraint by the government in not arrogating to itself powers at the expense of Parliament.

Self-restraint by the executive in the guise of conventions has been the hallmark of the constitution and it is through the change or atrophy in conventions, i.e. the way in which the government and ministers behave, that fundamental alterations in the constitution have been made. Observing of conventions becomes a matter of political expediency rather than honour and the constitution is reduced to what happens rather than what ought to happen. This is most clearly seen in the context of ministerial responsibility. Lord Carrington's resignation over the invasion of the Falklands was the exception which proved the rule. Mr Lamont resigned as Chancellor of the Exchequer not because of the events of 'Black Wednesday', when Britain left the ERM, but months later when a scapegoat was demanded by the party for the failure of the government's policies. Similarly, where the personal conduct of ministers has come under attack they have resigned only when their embarrassment to the party has made their position untenable, rather than because their conduct was unbecoming to a minister.

More importantly, ministers, with the possible exception of Lord Carrington, no longer resign for mistakes made in their departments. The whole concept of ministerial responsibility and the relationship between ministers and civil servants has fundamentally changed. No longer do civil servants act anonymously and impartially behind the shield of ministerial responsibility. Their political neutrality is under threat by their being used for party political ends. The most spectacular example of this is still the Westland affair but this may soon be overshadowed by revelations from the Scott inquiry into arms exports to Iraq. Lord Callaghan, a former Prime Minister, thought that this was a consequence of one party being in office for so many years which was a unique situation (HC 390-II, 1992–93, p. 138 seq.). The danger of this development is that it removes one of the safeguards in the constitution, the provision of objective, dispassionate and impartial advice to the government.

A similar example of the lack of self-restraint by ministers is in the appointments to quangos, where there is evidence of political patronage. These bodies which include the regulators of the privatized industries, urban development corporations and national health service trusts, raise fundamental issues of accountability. So far as they are independent and at arm's length from the government they represent a counter-balance to the power of the central government but the price paid for this is the lack of political accountability. This circle can never be squared but to politicize such bodies is to increase political power without responsibility.

The emasculation of local government through tight financial constraints on the one hand and privatization of services in its various forms on the other hand has increased the central government's powers and greatly diminished the only countervailing power exercised by directly elected bodies apart from the House of Commons. This profoundly affects the balance in the constitution especially in the absence of devolution to the countries and regions of the UK.

To what extent has this tilting of the balance of power in favour of the central government been countered by the shedding of government functions and empowerment of the individual? Privatization has been the main instrument to further this objective whilst the Citizen's Charter applies the philosophy of the private sector to the remaining public services and the privatized utilities. The citizen is seen as a customer of public services whether provided by the civil service, the executive agencies, the National Health Service, local authorities, private contractors or privatized utilities. The aim is efficient, cost-effective services and redress where they fall short of this ideal. What the Charter omits is perhaps more revealing than its content.

Consultation is referred to in the Charter as well as in consultation documents relating to parish councils and the police but the government's record on consultation is not exemplary. Consultation on legislation has often been cursory and at inconvenient times for those affected, whilst the lack of consultation over the banning of trade unions at GCHQ and over pit closures ended in the courts. In the spirit of the Citizen's Charter the government has committed itself to the provision of more information and openness and has taken some steps in this direction but it opposed the Right to Know Bill which would have gone considerably further.

There is no recognition in the Charter of the possibility of conflict between efficiency and fairness, a problem which is becoming increasingly worrying. There are now a number of cases where public inquiries are being dispensed with in the interests of efficiency where they were formerly obligatory, e.g.

local government restructuring and amalgamation of police authorities. The Council on Tribunals had to fight for the retention of the right to an inquiry in the case of planning appeals. The Council has also been concerned about dispensing with tribunals or watering down appeal procedures in the interests of economy and efficiency. They have expressed a warning about creating executive agencies which also have a judicial role, e.g. the Criminal Injuries Compensation Board (Report for 1991–2). Also executive agencies may be tempted to cut corners to meet their targets rather than be guided by the civil service values of equity and fairness. This problem will become more acute if executive agencies are privatized.

It is also revealing that there is no mention in the Charter of civil liberties. The state of civil liberties in Britain is not healthy. The inner-city riots in the early 1980s coupled with the miners' strike and other disturbances led to the passing of the Public Order Act 1986 which gives greater powers to the police to deal with meetings and processions to prevent disorder and disturbance. These have been vastly increased by the Criminal Justice and Public Order Bill 1994. Dissatisfaction with the criminal justice system led to the setting up of a Royal Commission in 1978 whose recommendations were largely implemented in the Police and Criminal Evidence Act 1984. The startling miscarriages of justice which came to light in the late 1980s led to another Royal Commission only ten years later. One of its main recommendations, to retain the right to silence, has been rejected by the government. The revelations about the security services in the book *Spycatcher* and elsewhere brought about a new Official Secrets Act in 1989 and the placing of the Security Services on a statutory basis in the Security Service Act 1989 and the Intelligence Services Act 1994. These Acts and their predecessor, the Interception of Communications Act 1985 dealing with telephone tapping, have not allayed fears about the activities of the security services.

The UK has the worst record in the European Court of Human Rights apart from Italy. This has fuelled the call for the enactment of the European Convention on Human Rights in the UK. This would involve the judges in interpreting very broad provisions and applying them to highly politically controversial issues. The danger is that they would be dragged into the political arena and that their impartiality would be called into question.

The courts are already being called on to decide very politically controversial issues but in the context of the existing law, in particular applying principles of judicial review. This has not so far embroiled them in political controversy. The House of Lords have held the Home Secretary to be in contempt for not complying with an order of a court, the first time that a minister has been found in contempt of court (*M v. Home Office*, 1993). The courts have frequently been asked to adjudicate in the conflicts between central and local government. They had to rule on the legality of telephone tapping (*Malone*, 1979 and *Ruddock*, 1987) and the publication of the book *Spycatcher* (1988) as well as the banning of trade unions from GCHQ (1984). More recently they were asked to determine the legality of pit closures by the Coal Board (1992) and the legality of ratifying the Maastricht Treaty (1993). Above all they had to decide whether an Act of Parliament passed in contravention of European Community law should be set aside. This involved adjudicating on the most fundamental principle of the constitution, the sovereignty of Parliament. The House of Lords held in *R. v. Secretary of State for Transport ex parte Factortame Ltd* (1990) that Parliament had fettered its sovereignty by the European Communities Act 1972 which gave precedence to European Community law over UK law and thus bound future Parliaments. This case rather than the challenge to the Maastricht Treaty is probably the most important constitutional case for 300 years.

It is European Community law which will increasingly operate over a wider area. This was at the heart of the debate over the Maastricht Treaty. The Conservative rebels were opposed to the further loss of parliamentary sovereignty, particularly in the area of economic policy. This was their central argument for a referendum to be held on the Treaty (HC Deb., vol. 223, col. 383 seq., 21 April 1993). The paradox was pointed out by their opponents, that a referendum was itself a diminution of parliamentary sovereignty. It has always been the main argument against a referendum that it is not in keeping with the traditions of a parliamentary democracy. This has not, however, prevented resort to a referendum by the Labour government in 1975 on the decision of whether to remain in the European Community and in 1979 on devolution to Scotland and Wales. They were both issues on which there were deep divisions within the Labour party, and the government could be said to have been appealing to the people in order to heal this split. A referendum was also held in respect of the Northern Ireland border in 1973. The special circumstance which existed in the case of the Maastricht Treaty was the unanimity of all three major parties in supporting the Treaty, so that at the 1992 General Election the voter was deprived of an opportunity to vote against the Treaty. This was Lord Blake's strongest argument in favour of a referendum but the House of Lords defeated the proposal by 445 votes to 176 (HL Deb., vol. 548, col. 239 seq., 14 July 1993), the biggest attendance of peers ever mobilized.

It is not only the Maastricht Treaty which has recently given rise to calls for a referendum. The Labour party has proposed that a referendum should be held on electoral reform and the Leader of the Liberal Democrat party has proposed advisory referenda in local and national government, if 1½% of the electorate demanded one, to enable ordinary people to feel more involved in the political process (*Guardian*, 29 July 1993). Such a proposal for a form of direct democracy requires a great deal of faith in the people. It was lack of trust in the people which Mr Shepherd was castigating when he spoke of seeking merely acquiescence not consent in the context of the Maastricht Treaty.

What needs to be done, therefore, to restore faith in our democratic institutions? The government argues that there is no need for constitutional reform since it has strengthened democracy by diminishing the role of the state and applying the ideology of the market to what is left of the public sector (*Guardian*, 7 July 1993, 'Waldegrave hits at reform lobby'). At the other end of the spectrum fundamental constitutional reforms such as proportional representation, devolution, referenda, a Bill of Rights and a written constitution have been recommended.

Conclusion

There is a middle way. It involves restoring the checks and balances of the constitution. This could be done without fundamental reforms if MPs asserted themselves more and governments exercised more self-restraint. If governments explained themselves better and listened more there could be greater scope for government by consent rather than acquiescence. Rousseau's gibe on British democracy over 200 years ago seems uncannily topical; 'The people of England', he wrote, 'regards itself as free but it is grossly mistaken; it is free only during the election of members of Parliament. As soon as they are elected, slavery overtakes it, and it is nothing. The use it makes of the short moments of liberty it enjoys shows indeed that it deserves to lose them' (The Social Contract, Book III, Chapter XV).

BIBLIOGRAPHY

Amery, L. S. (1953), *Thoughts on the Constitution*, second edition, Oxford: Oxford University Press.

Bagehot, W. (1963), *The English Constitution* (first edition 1867), London: Fontana.

Baker, D., Gamble, A. and Ludlam, S. (1993), 'Whips or Scorpions? The Maastricht Vote and the Conservative Party', *Parliamentary Affairs*, p. 151.

Bell, K. (1975), *Research Study on Supplementary Benefit Appeal Tribunals*, London: HMSO.

Benn, A. (1980), 'The Case for the Constitutional Premiership', *Parliamentary Affairs*, p. 7.

Boyle, Lord. (1980), 'Ministers and the Administrative Process', *Public Administration*, p. 1.

Brazier, R. (1991), *Constitutional Reform*, Oxford: Clarendon Press.

Crossman, R. (1975), *The Diaries of a Cabinet Minister*, London: Jonathan Cape.

Dicey, A. V. (1939), *Law of the Constitution* (first edition 1885), London: Macmillan.

Doig, A. (1993), 'The Double Whammy: The Resignation of David Mellor, MP', *Parliamentary Affairs*, p. 167.

Finer, S. E. (1956) 'Individual Responsibility of Ministers', *Public Administration*, p. 377.

Ganz, G. (1974), *Administrative Procedures*, London: Sweet and Maxwell.

Ganz, G. (1990), 'Recent Developments in the Use of Guillotine Motions, *Public Law*, p. 496.

Ganz, G. (1992), 'The War Crimes Act 1991 – Why No Constitutional Crisis?', *Modern Law Review*, p. 87.

Genn, H. (1993), 'Tribunals and Informal Justice', *Modern Law Review*, p. 393.

139

Hailsham, Lord. (1976), 'Elective Dictatorship', *Listener*, 21 October.

Hansard Society (1976), *Report of the Hansard Society Commission on Electoral Reform*, London: The Hansard Society.

Hansard Society (1992), *Making the Law: Report of the Hansard Society Commission on The Legislative Process*, London: The Hansard Society.

Harlow, C. and Rawlings, R. (1984), *Law and Administration*, London: Weidenfeld and Nicolson.

Institute for Public Policy Research (1991), *The Constitution of the United Kingdom*, London: Institute for Public Policy Research.

Jenkins, R. (1979), 'Home Thoughts from Abroad', *Listener*, 29 November.

Mackintosh, J. (1977), *The British Cabinet*, third edition, London: Sweet & Maxwell.

Mount, F. (1992), *The British Constitution Now*, London: Heinemann.

National Economic Development Office (1976), *A Study of UK Nationalised Industries*, London: HMSO.

Norton, P. (1982), *The Constitution in Flux*, Oxford: Martin Robertson.

Oliver, D. (1991), *Government in the United Kingdom*, Milton Keynes: Open University Press.

Outer Circle Policy Unit (1979), *The Big Public Inquiry*, London: Outer Circle Policy Unit.

Plant, Lord. (1991), *Democracy, Representation and Elections: First Report of the Working Party on Electoral Systems*, London: The Labour Party.

Plant, Lord (1993), *Third Report of the Working Party on Electoral Systems*, London: The Labour Party.

Ryle, M. and Richards, P. G. (1988), *The Communs under Scrutiny*, third edition, London: Routledge.

Scarman, Lord. (1985), 'The Shifting State: Public Administration in a Time of Change', *Public Administration*, p. 1.

Shell, D. (1985), 'The House of Lords and the Thatcher Government', *Parliamentary Affairs*, p. 16.

Shell, D. (1992), *The House of Lords*, second edition, London: Harvester Wheatsheaf.

Walker, D. (1990), 'Enter the Regulators', *Parliamentary Affairs*, p. 149.

Wass, Sir D. (1983), *The Reith Lectures*, London: BBC.

Zander, M. (1990), The Police and Criminal Evidence Act 1984, second edition, London: Sweet & Maxwell.

CASES

Numbers in bold refer to pages in the text

TABLE OF STATUTES

145

INDEX